Your Ray of
Hope for Today

Your Ray of *Hope* for Today

Devotional

PASTOR RAY SHANKLIN

iUniverse, Inc.
Bloomington

Your Ray of Hope for Today
Devotional

iUniverse books may be ordered through booksellers or by contacting:

iUniverse
1663 Liberty Drive
Bloomington, IN 47403
www.iuniverse.com
1-800-Authors (1-800-288-4677)

ISBN: 978-1-4697-4711-8 (sc)
ISBN: 978-1-4697-4712-5 (ebk)

Printed in the United States of America

iUniverse rev. date: 01/26/2012

DEDICATION

This book is dedicated to Helen, my loving wife of 62 years
(she went home to be with the Lord August 30,2006)

Also to our children, Gary and Doug

Then to our Grand children, Josh, Stacey, Jill,
Christian and Stephen

And to our great Grand Children, Gracie, Elle Anna,
Karston, Jeremiah, Madelynn
Brayden, and Ella Raye

And to my Mother, Edith Fay Allen

HAPPY NEW YEAR

JANUARY 1

STAY FREE

John 8:36

36 If the Son therefore shall make you free, ye shall be free indeed. Gal 4:99 But now, after that ye have known God, or rather are known of God, how turn ye again to the weak and beggarly elements, whereunto ye desire again to be in bondage? KJV

Jesus has set us free from the bondage of this world, it up to us to stay in that freedom and protect it. He will not take it from us, but we can take ourselves out of the freedom and back into the bondage from which we escaped. The choice is ours.

MAKE IT YOUR COMMITMENT TO STAY STRONG AND FREE IN THE NEW YEAR.

MAY GOD GRANT YOU A SAFE, HAPPY, AND PROSPEROUS YEAR.

"IN GOD WE TRUST"

Pastor Ray

JANUARY 2

THERE IS A TIME FOR EVERYTHING

Eccl 3:1-2,4,8

To every thing there is a season, and a time to every purpose under the heaven: **2** A time to be born, and a time to die; a time to plant, and a time to pluck up that which is planted; **4** A time to weep, and a time to laugh; a time to mourn, and a time to dance; **8** A time to love, and a time to hate; a time of war, and a time of peace. KJV

The right time for everything will be revealed to us through the Holy Spirit of God, and when we are on His time schedule everything will be right. So let us look forward to this year as a year to rebuild and restore what the devil has stolen from us. (James 4:7 KJV) Submit yourselves therefore to God. Resist the devil, and he will flee from you.

BE COMMITTED TO GOD AND RESIST YOUR ENEMIES,

VICTORY IS YOURS.

"IN GOD WE TRUST"

Pastor Ray

JANUARY 3

YOU ARE OF GREAT VALUE

Matt 10:29-31

29 Are not two sparrows sold for a farthing? and one of them shall not fall on the ground without your Father. **30** But the very hairs of your head are all numbered. **31** Fear ye not therefore, ye are of more value than many sparrows. KJV

You are more valuable to God then all the sparrows, and canaries combined, He even knows how many hairs you had on your head when you had a full head of hair, and will restore it when we get to Heaven too spend eternity with Him. His love for you is never ending.

CHEER UP JESUS HAS OVERCOME THE WORLD.

"IN GOD WE TRUST"

Pastor Ray

JANUARY 4

FOR YOU, THERE IS GREAT LOVE

John 3:11-16

11 Verily, verily, I say unto thee, We speak that we do know, and testify that we have seen; and ye receive not our witness. **12** If I have told you earthly things, and ye believe not, how shall ye believe, if I tell you of heavenly things? **13** And no man hath ascended up to heaven, but he that came down from heaven, even the Son of man which is in heaven. **14** And as Moses lifted up the serpent in the wilderness, even so must the Son of man be lifted up: **15** That whosoever believeth in him should not perish, but have eternal life. **16** For God so loved the world, that he gave his only begotten Son, that whosoever believeth in him should not perish, but have everlasting life. KJV

How great the love of God is for you. If you want to know how much Jesus loves you? Get a good mental picture of Him on the cross with His arms stretched as far as possible. As He said, to you, (With His arms stretched wide, nailed to the cross), this much, and died for you. He took all our sins and infirmities with Him, for He paid a price for us that we could never pay.

BE THANKFUL, AND HAVE GOOD SAFE DAY

"IN GOD WE TRUST"

Pastor Ray

JANUARY 5

JOY COMES IN THE MORNING

Psalm 30:4-5

4 Sing unto the LORD, O ye saints of his, and give thanks at the remembrance of his holiness. 5 For his anger endureth but a moment; in his favour is life: weeping may endure for a night, but joy cometh in the morning.

The King James Version, (Cambridge: Cambridge) 1769.

God will see you through, it doesn't matter how bad the situation, or how deep the valley, he will bring you through the night into daylight. For your joy comes in the morning.

SMILE, GOD LOVES YOU, HAVE A GREAT AND JOYFUL DAY.

"IN GOD WE TRUST"

Pastor Ray

JANUARY 6

FEAR NOT

Rev 1:17-18

17 And when I saw him, I fell at his feet as dead. And he laid his right hand upon me, saying unto me, Fear not; I am the first and the last: **18** I am he that liveth, and was dead; and, behold, I am alive for evermore, Amen; and have the keys of hell and of death. KJV

Fear not, is what God would say to you, for He knows that fear activates the devil and that faith will activates Himself (God). A saying to remember, especially in these times.

FEAR KNOCKED AT THE DOOR, FAITH ANSWERED AND THERE WAS NO ONE THERE.

HAVE A SAFE, AND BEAUTIFUL DAY.

"IN GOD WE TRUST"

JANUARY 7

IS ANYTHING TO HARD FOR GOD?

Gen 18:13-14

13 Then the Lord said to Abraham, "Why did Sarah laugh and say, 'Will I really have a child, now that I am old?' **14** Is anything too hard for the Lord? I will return to you at the appointed time next year and Sarah will have a son." NIV

If God can work this kind of miracle with a couple in there 90s, then surely our problems are a simple task for Him, but we have to give them to Him and leave them with Him before He can do anything with them. In other words don't take them back in five seconds if He hasn't done anything yet.

REMEMBER, GOD IS WORKING WITH PEOPLE, AND THEY ARE NOT ALL OBEDIENT.

HAVE A GREAT DAY.

"IN GOD WE TRUST"

Pastor Ray

JANUARY 8

THE GRACE OF GOD IS FOR YOU

Ps 84:10-12

10 For a day in thy courts is better than a thousand. I had rather be a doorkeeper in the house of my God, than to dwell in the tents of wickedness. **11** For the Lord God is a sun and shield: the Lord will give grace and glory: no good thing will he withhold from them that walk uprightly. **12** O Lord of hosts, blessed is the man that trusteth in thee. KJV

What is our part? To do what is right in the sight of God, When we do we can expect God to shower us with His mercy, grace, and peace, while withholding no good thing from us. That is good news to me and I hope to you also, because when we do our part God will do His.

BE FAITHFUL TO WHAT GOD HAS CALLED YOU TO DO,

AND HAVE A GREAT DAY.

"IN GOD WE TRUST"

Pastor Ray

JANUARY 9

EVERYTHING IS GOING TO BE ALL RIGHT

Isa 43:2-4

2 When thou passest through the waters, I will be with thee; and through the rivers, they shall not overflow thee: when thou walkest through the fire, thou shalt not be burned; neither shall the flame kindle upon thee. **3** For I am the Lord thy God, the Holy One of Israel, thy Saviour: I gave Egypt for thy ransom, Ethiopia and Seba for thee. **4** Since thou wast precious in my sight, thou hast been honourable, and I have loved thee: therefore will I give men for thee, and people for thy life. KJV

No matter how discouraged, mixed up and confused you feel, remember God is with you, and everything is going to be all right, for He is in control, bringing you through to victory. So He can shower you with His Love, Kindness, and mercy. Cheer up,

GOD HAS EVERY THING IN CONTROL.

"IN GOD WE TRUST"

Pastor Ray

JANUARY 10

YOU ARE LOVED

3 John 2-4

2 Beloved, I wish above all things that thou mayest prosper and be in health, even as thy soul prospereth. **3** For I rejoiced greatly, when the brethren came and testified of the truth that is in thee, even as thou walkest in the truth. **4** I have no greater joy than to hear that my children walk in truth. KJV

Your are called beloved a dear friend and only the best is wished or prayed for you. Isn't it great to know that you are so highly thought of and cared for by God, that you are constantly thought of by God, and in your friends prayers, praying and believing the best for you. You truly don't know how many pray for you on a daily basis, but this you know, that God's love for you is unlimited, without reservation, flows abundantly toward you continually as we are told in. "John 15:15 I no longer call you servants, because a servant does not know his master's business. Instead, I have called you friends, for everything that I learned from my Father I have made known to you. NIV"

YOU ARE A FRIEND OF GOD'S.

"IN GOD WE TRUST"

JANUARY 11

OPPRESSION SHALL BE FAR FROM YOU, AND YOUR CHILDREN SHALL HAVE PEACE

Isa 54:13-15

13 And all thy children shall be taught of the Lord; and great shall be the peace of thy children. **14** In righteousness shalt thou be established: thou shalt be far from oppression; for thou shalt not fear: and from terror; for it shall not come near thee. **15** Behold, they shall surely gather together, but not by me: whosoever shall gather together against thee shall fall for thy sake. KJV

This is our promise from God, as fear attempts to grip the world, His promise says it will not come near us, and He is able and willing to keep His promises. Our part is to have faith in Him, and have no fear, for fear activates the devil, and faith activates God. "(Mark 11:22 And Jesus answering saith unto them, Have faith in God. KJV)"

JESUS WOULD NEVER TELL US TO DO SOMETHING THAT WE COULDN'T DO.

"IN GOD WE TRUST"

JANUARY 12

GOD IS ON HIS WAY TO YOU

Ps 12:5-6

5 For the oppression of the poor, for the sighing of the needy, now will I arise, saith the Lord; I will set him in safety from him that puffeth at him. **6** The words of the Lord are pure words: as silver tried in a furnace of earth, purified seven times. KJV

God is getting fed up with the ways of the wicked of the world, and is coming to help, to heal the lonely hearts, and restore peace, to set at liberty them that are bruised. it is time for the people to make up their minds which side they are on, God's or Satan's, There is no in between, and God is extending His mercy to any one who will accept it. "Deut 30:19, I call heaven and earth to record this day against you, that I have set before you life and death, blessing and cursing: therefore choose life, that both thou and thy seed may live: KJV"

THE CHOICE IS OURS, GOD RECOMMENDS LIFE. HAVE A PEACEFUL DAY.

"IN GOD WE TRUST"

JANUARY 13

TIRED? GOD WILL HELP

Psalm 103:2-5

2 Bless the LORD, O my soul, and forget not all his benefits: 3 Who forgiveth all thine iniquities; who healeth all thy diseases; 4 Who redeemeth thy life from destruction; who crowneth thee with lovingkindness and tender mercies; 5 Who satisfieth thy mouth with good things; so that thy youth is renewed like the eagle's. The King James Version, (Cambridge: Cambridge) 1769.

If we will truly believe that He is God and can do what He says He will do, then we can rest assured that our strength will be renewed, our iniquities are forgiven and our diseases are healed, and that we have a life worth living.

WHAT A REWARD FOR TRUSTING IN GOD

"IN GOD WE TRUST"

Pastor Ray

JANUARY 13

NEED A FRIEND?

Proverbs 18:24

24 A man that hath friends must shew himself friendly: and there is a friend that sticketh closer than a brother.

The King James Version, (Cambridge: Cambridge) 1769.

What a friend we have in Jesus, He really does stick closer to us than a brother. He will never leave us nor forsake us when things get rough. Psalm 23:4 in the message Bible, says, "I may walk through valleys as dark as death, but I won't be afraid. You are with me, and your shepherd's rod makes me feel safe."

MAKE THIS YOUR CONFESSION OF FAITH IN HIM.

"IN GOD WE TRUST"

Pastor Ray

JANUARY 14

HAVE FAITH IN GOD

Mark 11:22

22 And Jesus answering saith unto them, Have faith in God. (The King James Version, (Cambridge: Cambridge) 1769.)

Gal 5:4-6

4 Christ is become of no effect unto you, whosoever of you are justified by the law; ye are fallen from grace. 5 For we through the Spirit wait for the hope of righteousness by faith. 6 For in Jesus Christ neither circumcision availeth anything, nor uncircumcision; but faith which worketh by love. (KJV)

We have all received a measure of faith. Jesus is the author and finisher of our faith. But what is our part? The exercising and developing of a strong faith is left up to us. If we never use our faith it will remain just the measure we started with, but if we do our part, to exercise and train and work our faith it will become strong and productive, God will help us with it, if we have faith in Him, for faith works by love and God is love. Build your faith to full strength that it may remove the mountains in your life, whatever they may be.

HAVE FAITH IN GOD

"IN GOD WE TRUST"

Pastor Ray

January 15

LET GOD DRY YOUR TEARS

Ps 30:4-6

4 Sing unto the Lord, O ye saints of his, and give thanks at the remembrance of his holiness. **5** For his anger endureth but a moment; in his favour is life: weeping may endure for a night, but joy cometh in the morning. **6** And in my prosperity I said, I shall never be moved. (KJV)

God loves you, He wants to give you his shoulder to cry on that He may dry your tears, and see you through the night or dark time in your life bringing you out into light and joy. Joy comes with the light, or as the night turns into day.

REACH OUT TO HIM, ALLOW HIM TO CONSOLE YOU AND DRY YOUR TEARS.

"IN GOD WE TRUST"

Pastor Ray

JANUARY 16

YOU ARE FORGIVEN

Ps 103:2-5

2 Bless the Lord, O my soul, and forget not all his benefits: **3** Who forgiveth all thine iniquities; who healeth all thy diseases; **4** Who redeemeth thy life from destruction; who crowneth thee with lovingkindness and tender mercies; **5** Who satisfieth thy mouth with good things; so that thy youth is renewed like the eagle's. KJV

God not only forgives us, but He also forgets our sins. He then throws in a bonus of healing. Notice the KJV says all our iniquities are forgiven. Our part is to praise and thank Him for it, and hold no grudges against others, in others words forgive as He has forgiven you. If we will forgive as He forgives; Then we can expect the rest of His promise to be healed, and redeemed, and receive His crown of love and compassion.

LET GO; AND LET GOD.

"IN GOD WE TRUST"

Pastor Ray

JANUARY 17

THE LORD IS YOUR HELPER

Ps 18:16-19

16 He sent from above, he took me, he drew me out of many waters. **17** He delivered me from my strong enemy, and from them which hated me: for they were too strong for me. **18** They prevented me in the day of my calamity: but the Lord was my stay. **19** He brought me forth also into a large place; he delivered me, because he delighted in me. KJV

When you pray for help, no matter where you are, God hears your cry and comes to help you through to victory, but we must be willing to open our heart and let Him in, as He will not force His way upon you. when He comes roll your cares over on Him and leave them there.

WALK WITH GOD, AND HAVE A BEAUTIFUL DAY.

"IN GOD WE TRUST"

JANUARY 18

DO YOU KNOW WHICH ROAD TO TAKE?

Ps 19:7-8

7 The law of the Lord is perfect, converting the soul: the testimony of the Lord is sure, making wise the simple. **8** The statutes of the Lord are right, rejoicing the heart: the commandment of the Lord is pure, enlightening the eyes. (KJV)

God's ways are sure and proven to lead us in the right direction, down the right road that takes us home to heaven. As we travel with God we will not have to question which road is right, for each one will give us joy and peace, and we will know in our hearts that we are on the right path.

GOD'S IS EASY, AND HIS LOAD IS LIGHT.

"IN GOD WE TRUST"

Pastor Ray

JANUARY 19

WE ALL HAVE NEEDS

Phil 4:19-20

19 But my God shall supply all your need according to his riches in glory by Christ Jesus. **20** Now unto God and our Father be glory for ever and ever. Amen.

KJV

For us to receive we must believe that God is able to perform what He has promised. How do we do that? By putting faith with our belief, in other words, have faith in God. I know, its easier said than done, but the results is well worth the effort. For we must first believe that He is, and that He rewards those who diligently seek Him. If we do our part He will do His.

BE DILIGENT, AND HAVE A GOOD DAY

"IN GOD WE TRUST"

JANUARY 20

GRACE AND PEACE HAVE BEEN GIVEN TO YOU

2 Peter 1:2-4

2 Grace and peace be multiplied unto you through the knowledge of God, and of Jesus our Lord, 3 According as his divine power hath given unto us all things that pertain unto life and godliness, through the knowledge of him that hath called us to glory and virtue: 4 Whereby are given unto us exceeding great and precious promises: that by these ye might be partakers of the divine nature, having escaped the corruption that is in the world through lust. KJV

The better we get to know Him the more of His precious and exceeding great promises we will be able to receive, they are already given to us, if they are ours then we need to learn to receive them. You can't get money out of your checking account it you don't know how to write a check. Believe and receive the good life God wants you to have.

TAKE WHAT IS YOURS. HAVE A BEAUTIFUL AND PROSPEROUS DAY.

"IN GOD WE TRUST"

JANUARY 21

IS YOUR BURDEN TO HEAVY?

Matt 11:28-30

28 Come unto me, all ye that labour and are heavy laden, and I will give you rest. **29** Take my yoke upon you, and learn of me; for I am meek and lowly in heart: and ye shall find rest unto your souls. **30** For my yoke is easy, and my burden is light. KJV

Let us lay our burden aside and take the burden He gives us, for it is much lighter than the one we lay on ourselves. If we will pull with Him and let Him help us with our burden, we will find that He does most of the pulling and carrying.

LET GO AND LET GOD; HAVE A NICE AND EASY DAY.

"IN GOD WE TRUST"

JANUARY 22

YOU ARE NOT CONDEMNED

Rom 8:1-2

There is therefore now no condemnation to them which are in Christ Jesus, who walk not after the flesh, but after the Spirit. **2** For the law of the Spirit of life in Christ Jesus hath made me free from the law of sin and death. KJV

God's Word will convict us of our sins, but will never condemn us. When we are convicted of our sins and confess them to God He is quick to forgive and forget, immediately we are cleansed. In other words we have nothing to be condemned for, He no longer remembers our sins, for Jesus has paid for them and forgotten them. Our responsibility is to stay hooked up with Jesus, giving Him control of our lives. In other words.

SOLD OUT TO HIM AND HIS WAYS. HAVE AN ENJOYABLE DAY.

"IN GOD WE TRUST"

JANUARY 23

SPEAK TO YOUR MOUNTAIN

Mark 11:22-26

22 And Jesus answering saith unto them, Have faith in God. **23** For verily I say unto you, That whosoever shall say unto this mountain, Be thou removed, and be thou cast into the sea; and shall not doubt in his heart, but shall believe that those things which he saith shall come to pass; he shall have whatsoever he saith. **24** Therefore I say unto you, What things soever ye desire, when ye pray, believe that ye receive them, and ye shall have them. **25** And when ye stand praying, forgive, if ye have ought against any: that your Father also which is in heaven may forgive you your trespasses. **26** But if ye do not forgive, neither will your Father which is in heaven forgive your trespasses. KJV

What is your mountain? Debt, loneliness, grief, sickness, relationships, whatever it is speak to it in faith believing in Jesus name, believe with all your heart in Gods ability to remove the mountain. Then you can prayerfully thank Him for it until you see the manifestation of its removal. If we will do our part, (have faith in God) God will do His part.

GOD MIGHT SAY IT THIS WAY, "YOU DO AND I WILL, YOU DON'T AND I WONT."

WALK IN FORGIVENESS AND HAVE A GREAT DAY.

"IN GOD WE TRUST"

JANUARY 24

PRIORITIES, WHAT ARE YOURS?

Matt 6:30-33

30 Wherefore, if God so clothe the grass of the field, which to day is, and tomorrow is cast into the oven, shall he not much more clothe you, O ye of little faith? **31** Therefore take no thought, saying, What shall we eat? or, What shall we drink? or, Wherewithal shall we be clothed? **32** (For after all these things do the Gentiles seek:) for your heavenly Father knoweth that ye have need of all these things. **33** But seek ye first the kingdom of God, and his righteousness; and all these things shall be added unto you. KJV

If we can only come to the place in our life where we can truly put God in first place, then everything we need, pertaining to life and godliness will be provided, If we will make God our number one priority, He will make us His number one priority showering us with His love and blessings.

HONOR GOD, AND HE WILL HONOR YOU.

"IN GOD WE TRUST"

Pastor Ray

JANUARY 25

GIVE THANKS WITH PRAISE

Ps 150

Praise ye the Lord. Praise God in his sanctuary: praise him in the firmament of his power. **2** Praise him for his mighty acts: praise him according to his excellent greatness. **3** Praise him with the sound of the trumpet: praise him with the psaltery and harp. **4** Praise him with the timbrel and dance: praise him with stringed instruments and organs. **5** Praise him upon the loud cymbals: praise him upon the high sounding cymbals. **6** Let every thing that hath breath praise the Lord. Praise ye the Lord. KJV

We should be very thankful and praise Him with joy for what He has done for us.

PRAISE GOD AS YOU WALK THROUGH YOUR DAYS, AND ENJOY THEM.

"IN GOD WE TRUST"

JANUARY 26

YOU ARE PRECIOUS

Isa 13:11-13

11 And I will punish the world for their evil, and the wicked for their iniquity; and I will cause the arrogancy of the proud to cease, and will lay low the haughtiness of the terrible. **12** I will make a man more precious than fine gold; even a man than the golden wedge of Ophir. **13** Therefore I will shake the heavens, and the earth shall remove out of her place, in the wrath of the Lord of hosts, and in the day of his fierce anger.

KJV

You are precious to God, He choose you to be His own, He knew what you were like, but He loved you and choose you just the way you were, He did not ask you to clean up and get rid of your sins before He took you into His family. He accepted you just the way you were, and then began the clean up process, to bring you into a precious relationship with Him.

WALK UPRIGHTLY BEFORE HIM, DON'T STIR UP HIS ANGER, AND HAVE A GREAT DAY.

"IN GOD WE TRUST"

Pastor Ray

JANUARY 27

THIS IS YOUR DAY

Ps 118:21-25

21 I will praise thee: for thou hast heard me, and art become my salvation. **22** The stone which the builders refused is become the head stone of the corner. **23** This is the Lord's doing; it is marvellous in our eyes. **24** This is the day which the Lord hath made; we will rejoice and be glad in it. **25** Save now, I beseech thee, O Lord: O Lord, I beseech thee, send now prosperity. KJV

Every day is the day He has made and we should expect great things from Him. We can rejoice in the gifts we receive from Him, from the little ones like a good parking space in a crowded lot, or an auto air conditioner repair that only cost nine cents and took less than 5 minutes, or a major thing like good health, salvation, the restoration of a relationship, or financial needs met. For this is a day He has made for us to be glad and rejoice in.

PURPOSE IN YOUR HEART AND MIND TO REJOICE, AND HAVE A *GREAT DAY.*

"IN GOD WE TRUST"

Pastor Ray

JANUARY 28

HIS MERCY ENDURES FOREVER

Ps 100

Make a joyful noise unto the Lord, all ye lands. **2** Serve the Lord with gladness: come before his presence with singing. **3** Know ye that the Lord he is God: it is he that hath made us, and not we ourselves; we are his people, and the sheep of his pasture. **4** Enter into his gates with thanksgiving, and into his courts with praise: be thankful unto him, and bless his name. **5** For the Lord is good; his mercy is everlasting; and his truth endureth to all generations. KJV

It is good to be on the receiving end of Gods goodness and His mercy. I thank Him continually for the goodness and mercy He extends to us and to you daily. I was just reminiscing yesterday how good God has been to us and our family over our life time, and throughout our marriage. If she were still here we would have celebrated our 65th anniversary yesterday the 28th of January. May God bless you all with His goodness and mercy as you go through your life with Him.

ENJOY THE TRIP, HAVE A GREAT DAY.

"IN GOD WE TRUST"

JANUARY 29

HOW TO HAVE MORE THAN ENOUGH

2 Corinthians 9:6-8

6 But this I say, He which soweth sparingly shall reap also sparingly; and he which soweth bountifully shall reap also bountifully. 7 Every man according as he purposeth in his heart, so let him give; not grudgingly, or of necessity: for God loveth a cheerful giver. 8 And God is able to make all grace abound toward you; that ye, always having all sufficiency in all things, may abound to every good work: KJV

Sow cheerfully some of what you have need of, Love, Friendship, help, money, kindness, joy, compassion, etc. Pray for others to also receive what you have need of, if healing then pray for someone who you know needs healing. Then God will generously supply you with all you need. The friendlier we are with others the more friendly folks will be with us. Don't eat your seed or store it up for safe keeping.

SOW YOUR SEED AND WATCH IT GROW, HAVE A BEAUTIFUL DAY.

"IN GOD WE TRUST"

Pastor Ray

JANUARY 30

NOTHING CAN SEPARATE YOU FROM GOD'S LOVE

Romans 8:38-39

38 For I am persuaded, that neither death, nor life, nor angels, nor principalities, nor powers, nor things present, nor things to come, 39 Nor height, nor depth, nor any other creature, shall be able to separate us from the love of God, which is in Christ Jesus our Lord. KJV

The love of God for you is so deep, and wide, yet it is centered on just you. There is no possible way for anything to stop that love from coming to you except yourself, you can refuse to receive God's love, for He will not force you to do anything you don't want to do, yet his love is directed to you at all times, waiting for you to open you heart and receive, for in today's times we need His love more than ever before.

OPEN YOUR HEART AND LET LOVE IN, THEN HAVE A HAPPY DAY.

"IN GOD WE TRUST"

JANUARY 31

DO YOU HAVE HEARTS DESIRES?

Psalm 37:3-5

3 Trust in the LORD, and do good; so shalt thou dwell in the land, and verily thou shalt be fed. 4 Delight thyself also in the LORD; and he shall give thee the desires of thine heart. 5 Commit thy way unto the LORD; trust also in him; and he shall bring it to pass. KJV

let us all follow these scriptures and commit everything we do to the Lord. Trusting Him to help us. This is a hard thing for most of us too do, especially when we have great needs or hurts, as we seem to have the attitude that we can do it better and quicker. Lets give it to Him and leave it there, trusting Him with all our heart, to give us our hearts desires.

YOU CAN RECEIVE YOUR HEARTS DESIRES. MAY YOUR DAY BE GREAT AND PROSPEROUS.

"IN GOD WE TRUST"

FEBRUARY 1

YOUR HELPER IS ONLY A PRAYER AWAY

Isaiah 41:10

10 Fear thou not; for I am with thee: be not dismayed; for I am thy God: I will strengthen thee; yea, I will help thee; yea, I will uphold thee with the right hand of my righteousness. KJV

God is telling us that He will help us and uphold us, But we must ask Him, as He will never force Himself on anyone, His love for us is without reservations as He is no respecter of persons, and He is not a man that He should lie. He will do for you all what He has done for one, if we will only ask in prayer, and believe that He will fulfill these scriptures for us.

BELIEVE AND RECEIVE, GOD IS WITH YOU, HAVE A GREAT DAY.

"IN GOD WE TRUST"

Pastor Ray

FEBRUARY 2

GIVE THANKS WITH PRAISE

Ps 150:1-2, 6

Praise ye the Lord. Praise God in his sanctuary: praise him in the firmament of his power. **2** Praise him for his mighty acts: praise him according to his excellent greatness. **6** Let every thing that hath breath praise the Lord. Praise ye the Lord. KJV

We should be very thankful and praise Him with joy for what He has done for us.

SHOUT YOUR VICTORY IN PRAISE, ENJOY YOUR DAY

"IN GOD WE TRUST"

Pastor Ray

FEBRUARY 3

WATCH AND PRAY

Matt 26:38-41

38 Then saith he unto them, My soul is exceeding sorrowful, even unto death: tarry ye here, and watch with me. **39** And he went a little further, and fell on his face, and prayed, saying, O my Father, if it be possible, let this cup pass from me: nevertheless not as I will, but as thou wilt. **40** And he cometh unto the disciples, and findeth them asleep, and saith unto Peter, What, could ye not watch with me one hour? **41** Watch and pray, that ye enter not into temptation: the spirit indeed is willing, but the flesh is weak. KJV

Watch out for temptation and pray against them as our flesh is usually to weak to resist even though our spirit may be strong, God has promised that there would be no temptation to great, for He will provide us with a way out.

JESUS IS YOUR WAY OUT. HAVE A GREAT DAY IN HIM.

"IN GOD WE TRUST"

Pastor Ray

FEBRUARY 4

WALK IN FORGIVENESS

Matt 6:14-15

14 For if ye forgive men their trespasses, your heavenly Father will also forgive you: **15** But if ye forgive not men their trespasses, neither will your Father forgive your trespasses. KJV

Forgiveness is like a medicine to our spirit man, when we take the first step and forgive those who have hurt us, it opens the door of our heart to let God's forgiveness flow to us, lets Him flood us with His love, which begins to remove bitterness and hatred, which causes sickness in our bodies.

WALK IN FORGIVENESS AND LET GOD SET YOU FREE, ENJOY YOUR FREEDOM BEGINNING TODAY.

"IN GOD WE TRUST"

FEBRUARY 5

TROUBLED?

2 Cor 4:7-9

7 But we have this treasure in earthen vessels, that the excellency of the power may be of God, and not of us. **8** We are troubled on every side, yet not distressed; we are perplexed, but not in despair; **9** Persecuted, but not forsaken; cast down, but not destroyed; KJV

God is our constant companion, even when we don't think He is there, He promised He would never leave us or forsake us, and God never breaks a promise. We may get knocked down, but He is always there to help whatever the trouble may be, always ready to lift you up and set your feet on solid ground. Trust and rely on Him.

HE WILL UPHOLD YOU WITH HIS RIGHTEOUS RIGHT HAND. HAVE A HAPPY DAY.

"IN GOD WE TRUST"

In His Love
Pastor Ray

FEBRUARY 6

YOU ARE AN OVERCOMER!

1 John 4:4-6

4 Ye are of God, little children, and have overcome them: because greater is he that is in you, than he that is in the world. **5** They are of the world: therefore speak they of the world, and the world heareth them. **6** We are of God: he that knoweth God heareth us; he that is not of God heareth not us. Hereby know we the spirit of truth, and the spirit of error. KJV

Notice the word "have" is past tense, which is telling us that because those that are born again into Gods family have already conquered the enemies of God. Because the Spirit of God is residence in you, and is stronger than the spirits that are in the world, like the spirit of fear that causes you to fear cancer, poverty, sickness and death, it is an enemy of God and you have already overcome it.

WALK IN VICTORY, AND ENJOY YOUR DAY

"IN GOD WE TRUST"

Pastor Ray

FEBRUARY 7

DON'T KNOW WHERE TO TURN?

Prov 3:5-8

5 Trust in the Lord with all thine heart; and lean not unto thine own understanding. **6** In all thy ways acknowledge him, and he shall direct thy paths. **7** Be not wise in thine own eyes: fear the Lord, and depart from evil. **8** It shall be health to thy navel, and marrow to thy bones. KJV

When we truly trust or lean on Him, then He can lead and heal without any hindrance on our part, His ways are proven and sure. We only get in trouble when we try to take the lead. Our impatience usually gets us onto the wrong track, we give our problems over to God, and if He doesn't have them taken care of in about 30 seconds, we reach out and take them back, and as long as we have them He can do nothing with them. As He will not override your authority, God will not make you do anything you do not want to, and the devil can't make you do anything you truly do not want to do.

GIVE GOD A CHANCE, AND HAVE A HEALTHY HAPPY DAY.

"IN GOD WE TRUST"

Pastor Ray

FEBRUARY 8

HOW TO MAKE A PROFIT AND LIVE WELL

Isa 48:15-17

15 I, even I, have spoken; yea, I have called him: I have brought him, and he shall make his way prosperous. **16** Come ye near unto me, hear ye this; I have not spoken in secret from the beginning; from the time that it was, there am I: and now the Lord God, and his Spirit, hath sent me. **17** Thus saith the Lord, thy Redeemer, the Holy One of Israel; I am the Lord thy God which teacheth thee to profit, which leadeth thee by the way that thou shouldest go. KJV

God can only teach you to profit and live well when you are willing to be taught, and He can only lead you when you are willing to follow. He will not force you, but will gently lead you into the right position at the right time for you to be successful.

LET GO AND LET GOD

"IN GOD WE TRUST"

Pastor Ray

FEBRUARY 9

RESISTING TEMPTATIONS

1 Corinthians 10:13

13 There hath no temptation taken you but such as is common to man: but God is faithful, who will not suffer you to be tempted above that ye are able; but will with the temptation also make a way to escape, that ye may be able to bear it.

The King James Version, (Cambridge: Cambridge) 1769.

God will always help us find a way to resist the temptations that we are faced with, most of the times we let ourselves get into a tempting situation, but God is faithful to his promise, He will always provide a way out, if we will accept it.

BELIEVE AND RECEIVE, HAVE A GREAT DAY

"IN GOD WE TRUST"

FEBRUARY 10

NOTHING IS TO HARD FOR GOD

Luke 1:37

37 For with God nothing shall be impossible.

The King James Version, (Cambridge: Cambridge) 1769.

This is one of the shortest verses in the scriptures, but it speaks volumes about Gods ability to help in time of need. It is hard to expand on this verse of scripture, but when we think there is no hope, and can't seem to figure out where we should go, God will show up, for nothing is impossible for God.

GOD IS WITH YOU, ENJOY YOUR DAY.

"IN GOD WE TRUST"

Pastor Ray

FEBRUARY 11

YOUR POWER OF ATTORNEY

John 14:11-14

11 Believe me that I am in the Father, and the Father in me: or else believe me for the very works' sake. **12** Verily, verily, I say unto you, He that believeth on me, the works that I do shall he do also; and greater works than these shall he do; because I go unto my Father. **13** And whatsoever ye shall ask in my name, that will I do, that the Father may be glorified in the Son. **14** If ye shall ask any thing in my name, I will do it. KJV

We are given the authority to use the name of Jesus in our time of need, we must remember to ask in His name, believe we receive in His name, and give thanks in His name. Do not hesitate to use the name of Jesus over ever situation, as His name is your power of attorney.

DON'T USE THE NAME OF JESUS IN VAIN.

"IN GOD WE TRUST"

Pastor Ray

FEBRUARY 12

KEEP YOUR DREAMS ALIVE

Mark 9:23

23 Jesus said unto him, If thou canst believe, all things are possible to him that believeth. KJV

Mark 9:23

23 Jesus replied, "Why do you say 'if you can'? Anything is possible for someone who has faith!"

The Contemporary English [computer file], electronic ed., Logos Library System, (Nashville: Thomas Nelson) 1997, c1995 by the American Bible Society.

If we will only believe and have faith in God, keeping our dreams alive, letting God direct our steps, walking constantly toward the completion of our dream.

ALL THINGS BECOME POSSIBLE

"IN GOD WE TRUST"

Pastor Ray

FEBRUARY 13

LOVE IS AN ACTION

Luke 6:27-30

27 But I say unto you which hear, Love your enemies, do good to them which hate you, **28** Bless them that curse you, and pray for them which despitefully use you. **29** And unto him that smiteth thee on the one cheek offer also the other; and him that taketh away thy cloke forbid not to take thy coat also. **30** Give to every man that asketh of thee; and of him that taketh away thy goods ask them not again. KJV

If we will take the action laid out for us in these scriptures we will receive the peace of God which is beyond our understanding. God is no respecter of persons, it worked for me and it will work for you. I began praying for a person whom I thought was despitefully using me and after a few years that person came to me and ask forgiveness, and became one of my most loyal friends. Peace and contentment is one thing we really need, especially in today's times.

FORGIVE AND YOU SHALL BE FORGIVEN.

"IN GOD WE TRUST"

Pastor Ray

FEBRUARY 14

OPPRESSION SHALL BE FAR FROM YOU

Isaiah 54:14

14 In righteousness shalt thou be established: thou shalt be far from oppression; for thou shalt not fear: and from terror; for it shall not come near thee.

The King James Version, (Cambridge: Cambridge) 1769.

This is our promise from God, and He is able and willing to keep His promises. Our part is to have faith in Him, trusting Him to do what He says,

AND HAVE FAITH IN YOURSELF

"IN GOD WE TRUST"

Pastor Ray

FEBRUARY 15

YOU ARE A VERY SPECIAL PERSON

John 15:16

16 Ye have not chosen me, but I have chosen you, and ordained you, that ye should go and bring forth fruit, and that your fruit should remain: that whatsoever ye shall ask of the Father in my name, he may give it you. KJV

You are chosen to produce the fruit of the Spirit in your life. Why? So that when you do, your prayers will be answered. The fruit of the Spirit is love, joy, peace, longsuffering, gentleness, goodness faith, meekness, temperance: against such there is no law.

YOU ARE A VERY SPECIAL PERSON

"IN GOD WE TRUST"

Pastor Ray

FEBRUARY 16

FEAR NOT

Genesis 50:21

21 Now therefore fear ye not: I will nourish you, and your little ones. And he comforted them, and spake kindly unto them.

The King James Version, (Cambridge: Cambridge) 1769.

God is reassuring us that He will take care of us and our children today just as He did the Hebrew Children. We must believe and be still to hear what He would have us do and know that He is God. Jesus would never tell us to do something that we couldn't do.

RECEIVE GODS HELP

"IN GOD WE TRUST"

Pastor Ray

FEBRUARY 17

THE CHOICE IS YOURS

Deut 30:19-20

19 I call heaven and earth to record this day against you, that I have set before you life and death, blessing and cursing: therefore choose life, that both thou and thy seed may live: **20** That thou mayest love the Lord thy God, and that thou mayest obey his voice, and that thou mayest cleave unto him: for he is thy life, and the length of thy days: that thou mayest dwell in the land which the Lord sware unto thy fathers, to Abraham, to Isaac, and to Jacob, to give them. KJV

We are given a multiple choice question between life death, blessing and curses. It dose not take a rocket scientist to know which one to choose, but just in case we can't make the right choice, we have been given the answer and the reward for getting it right. That we and our children can live a good life, a blessed life, without fear, having joy in our relationship with our heavenly Father.

REACH OUT TO GOD

"IN GOD WE TRUST"

Pastor Ray

FEBRUARY 18

DON'T TURN BACK, VICTORY IS NEAR

Galatians 4:8-9

8 Howbeit then, when ye knew not God, ye did service unto them which by nature are no gods. 9 But now, after that ye have known God, or rather are known of God, how turn ye again to the weak and beggarly elements, whereunto ye desire again to be in bondage? KJV

God knows us well, it wasn't when we confessed our sins that He found out about them, He was there when we did them, He also knows our desires, and lets us make the decision whether to stay with Him or go back to the things we came out of. So don't turn back you are almost to the finish line. There is joy and peace with Him, torment in the others.

THE CHOICE IS YOURS, PEACE OR TORMENT?

"IN GOD WE TRUST"

Pastor Ray

FEBRUARY 19

OBEDIENCE

1 Sam 15:22-23

22 And Samuel said, Hath the Lord as great delight in burnt offerings and sacrifices, as in obeying the voice of the Lord? Behold, to obey is better than sacrifice, and to hearken than the fat of rams. **23** For rebellion is as the sin of witchcraft, and stubbornness is as iniquity and idolatry. Because thou hast rejected the word of the Lord, he hath also rejected thee from being king. KJV

Our sacrifice is only pleasing to God when our hearts are right towards Him. He had much rather be able to talk with us and have us be obedient to what he moves us to do through the unction of His Holy Spirit than all the sacrifices we make. When God moves on my heart to pray for one or all of you, I need to be obedient right then, as after a while may be to late. If the prayer was not needed at that moment he would not have asked for it.

PRAY,HEAR, AND OBEY.

"IN GOD WE TRUST"

Pastor Ray

FEBRUARY 20

NEED HELP? HIS GRACE IS SUFFICIENT

2 Cor 12:7-10

7 And lest I should be exalted above measure through the abundance of the revelations, there was given to me a thorn in the flesh, the messenger of Satan to buffet me, lest I should be exalted above measure. **8** For this thing I besought the Lord thrice, that it might depart from me. **9** And he said unto me, My grace is sufficient for thee: for my strength is made perfect in weakness. Most gladly therefore will I rather glory in my infirmities, that the power of Christ may rest upon me. **10** Therefore I take pleasure in infirmities, in reproaches, in necessities, in persecutions, in distresses for Christ's sake: for when I am weak, then am I strong. KJV

If we can only come to the place in our life where we can truly trust God, and believe what He says in His word is for us today, then we will see Him do great things for us, When we are up against a wall, not knowing what to do, feeling so helpless, because we are to weak to help ourselves, if we will cry out to Jesus He will show His strength in our weakness.

HE DID IT FOR ME AND HE WILL DO IT FOR YOU.

"IN GOD WE TRUST"

Pastor Ray

FEBRUARY 21

SOMETHING BOTHERING YOU?

Zech 4:5-7

5 Then the angel that talked with me answered and said unto me, Knowest thou not what these be? And I said, No, my lord. **6** Then he answered and spake unto me, saying, This is the word of the Lord unto Zerubbabel, saying, Not by might, nor by power, but by my spirit, saith the Lord of hosts. **7** Who art thou, O great mountain? before Zerubbabel thou shalt become a plain: and he shall bring forth the headstone thereof with shoutings, crying, Grace, grace unto it. KJV

Make this a personal word from God to you by putting your name in the place of Zerubbabel. The Bible is God's personal message to us all, we should always let God handle the situation by His Spirit, rather than us trying to work our way through it without His help. It took me many years to learn this, but believe me it works.

WHAT EVER YOUR MOUNTAIN, PRAYER AND FAITH WILL MOVE IT.

"IN GOD WE TRUST"

Pastor Ray

FEBRUARY 22

ARE YOU UNDECIDED?

James 1:5-8

5 If any of you lack wisdom, let him ask of God, that giveth to all men liberally, and upbraideth not; and it shall be given him. **6** But let him ask in faith, nothing wavering. For he that wavereth is like a wave of the sea driven with the wind and tossed. **7** For let not that man think that he shall receive any thing of the Lord. **8** A double minded man is unstable in all his ways. KJV

God loves to have us ask Him what He would want us to do in every situation, we know that He hears us and gives us answers, our problem is that we don't always listen, and when we do, the answer we receive may not line up with what we think, so we set it aside and do our own thing, then get in trouble and cry out, why God? Let us ask, listen, and receive the wisdom of God.

PRAY, LISTEN, AND OBEY

"IN GOD WE TRUST"

Pastor Ray

FEBRUARY 23

GRACE AND PEACE OF GOD FOR YOU

2 Peter 1:2-4

2 Grace and peace be multiplied unto you through the knowledge of God, and of Jesus our Lord, **3** According as his divine power hath given unto us all things that pertain unto life and godliness, through the knowledge of him that hath called us to glory and virtue: **4** Whereby are given unto us exceeding great and precious promises: that by these ye might be partakers of the divine nature, having escaped the corruption that is in the world through lust. KJV

Grace and peace to you, His grace and peace is given to each of us out of His love, He has already given us everything we need, so let us also give Him everything He needs, our love and thanks, while we draw on our account that He has established for us. Everything pertaining to life and godliness.

CASH IN ON HIS GIFT. AND HAVE A GREAT DAY

"IN GOD WE TRUST"

February 24

ANSWERED PRAYER BRINGS JOY

Job 33:26-28

26 He shall pray unto God, and he will be favourable unto him: and he shall see his face with joy: for he will render unto man his righteousness. **27** He looketh upon men, and if any say, I have sinned, and perverted that which was right, and it profited me not; **28** He will deliver his soul from going into the pit, and his life shall see the light. KJV

God wants us to turn to Him not run from Him. His desire for us is to have a relationship with Him. He wishes to walk and talk with us. As we pray to Him in thanksgiving He gives us His righteousness, which gives us a new life and great joy.

WALK WITH GOD, AND HAVE A GREAT DAY

"IN GOD WE TRUST"

Pastor Ray

FEBRUARY 25

HIS DEFENSE IS YOUR JOY

Ps 5:11-12

11 But let all those that put their trust in thee rejoice: let them ever shout for joy, because thou defendest them: let them also that love thy name be joyful in thee. **12** For thou, Lord, wilt bless the righteous; with favour wilt thou compass him as with a shield. KJV

As we see His love manifested to us in His protection, we develop a trust in Him that brings internal joy that manifests in outward rejoicing.

YOU ARE PROTECTED

"IN GOD WE TRUST"

FEBRUARY 26

GOD KNOWS YOUR HEART

Ps 147:2-6

2 The Lord doth build up Jerusalem: he gathereth together the outcasts of Israel. **3** He healeth the broken in heart, and bindeth up their wounds. **4** He telleth the number of the stars; he calleth them all by their names. **5** Great is our Lord, and of great power: his understanding is infinite. **6** The Lord lifteth up the meek: he casteth the wicked down to the ground. KJV

God knows you better than you know yourself, He loves you and cares for you. When your heart aches so does His. Scripture tells us that He stands at the door (of our hearts) and knocks. If we will open the door He will come in and heal our broken hearts and soothe our wounds.

GIVE HIM A CHANCE TO LIFT YOU UP.

"IN GOD WE TRUST"

FEBRUARY 27

YOU HAVE A PLACE OF PROTECTION

Ps 91:1-4

He that dwelleth in the secret place of the most High shall abide under the shadow of the Almighty. **2** I will say of the Lord, He is my refuge and my fortress: my God; in him will I trust. **3** Surely he shall deliver thee from the snare of the fowler, and from the noisome pestilence. **4** He shall cover thee with his feathers, and under his wings shalt thou trust: his truth shall be thy shield and buckler.

KJV

It is comforting for us to know that we have a place to run to when we are in trouble, a place of safety, where we will be protected by a loving father we can trust, one who waits for us with open arms, someone we can confide in. Especially in times like these when it seems like our whole world is going crazy.

COME INTO YOUR PLACE OF PROTECTION.

"IN GOD WE TRUST"

FEBRUARY 28

FEAR NOTHING

Ps 91:5-8

5 Thou shalt not be afraid for the terror by night; nor for the arrow that flieth by day; **6** Nor for the pestilence that walketh in darkness; nor for the destruction that wasteth at noonday. **7** A thousand shall fall at thy side, and ten thousand at thy right hand; but it shall not come nigh thee. **8** Only with thine eyes shalt thou behold and see the reward of the wicked. KJV

this is Gods promise to you, if you will open your heart and invite Him in. All you have to do is say, "Jesus help" then surrender to Him and let Him have His way in your lives, but you have to make a firm decision to let Him in, you can not straddle the fence, keeping one foot in the world and the other in the kingdom of God.

BE DECISIVE, AND HAVE A HAPPY DAY.

"IN GOD WE TRUST"

Pastor Ray

MARCH 1

GOD HEARS YOUR PRAYERS

Psalm 66:16-20

16 Come and hear, all ye that fear God, and I will declare what he hath done for my soul. 17 I cried unto him with my mouth, and he was extolled with my tongue. 18 If I regard iniquity in my heart, the Lord will not hear me: 19 But verily God hath heard me; he hath attended to the voice of my prayer. 20 Blessed be God, which hath not turned away my prayer, nor his mercy from me. KJV

When we are at the end of our rope and have slipped past that last knot to hold on to, some times all we can do is cry "God please help me." He knows our hearts and is always faithful to hear and answer, He will deal with our condition later. He accepts us just the way we are, His love is unconditional. His forgiveness is instant the moment we cry out to Him, and He never goes back to condemn you. God really does hear your prayers.

PRAY, AND GIVE HIM A CHANCE TO ANSWER. HAVE A GREAT DAY.

"IN GOD WE TRUST"

Pastor Ray

MARCH 2

YOU ARE NOT CONDEMNED

Rom 8:1-2

There is therefore now no condemnation to them which are in Christ Jesus, who walk not after the flesh, but after the Spirit. **2** For the law of the Spirit of life in Christ Jesus hath made me free from the law of sin and death. KJV

God's Word will convict us of our sins, but will never condemn us. When we are convicted of our sins and confess them to God He is quick to forgive and forget them, immediately we are cleansed. In other words we have nothing to be condemned for, He remembers our sins no more. He sees us just the way we are, nothing is hidden from Him. It was not when we confessed our sins that He found out about them, He was there when we committed them.

LET HIM HANDLE THEM, AND HAVE A GOOD DAY

"IN GOD WE TRUST"

Pastor Ray

MARCH 3

A SPECIAL GIFT FOR YOU

Ephesians 2:8-10

8 For by grace are ye saved through faith; and that not of yourselves: it is the gift of God: 9 Not of works, lest any man should boast. 10 For we are his workmanship, created in Christ Jesus unto good works, which God hath before ordained that we should walk in them. KJV

You have been in Gods heart and on His mind since before you were conceived, He has loved you, and cared about you since the day you were born, and planed for your success and your future. However He will never force you to go His way, He always leaves the choice up to you.

MAKE A QUALITY DECISION, AND HAVE A GREAT DAY.

"IN GOD WE TRUST"

MARCH 4

FORGIVE AND LIVE IN QUITE PEACE

Ps 46:8-10

8 Come, behold the works of the Lord, what desolations he hath made in the earth. **9** He maketh wars to cease unto the end of the earth; he breaketh the bow, and cutteth the spear in sunder; he burneth the chariot in the fire. **10** Be still, and know that I am God: I will be exalted among the heathen, I will be exalted in the earth. KJV

It is a hard thing for us to be still and let God do His thing, our tendency is to take back what we have given him to handle, when in our opinion He is not getting it done fast enough. Think of the peace you will have when you have forgiven those that have harmed you. You can be at peace with yourself, with no grudges. Knowing that God can handle things better than you can. Forgive and let Him have and handle the problem.

PRAY AND LET GOD SHOW THE WAY, HAVE A GREAT DAY

"IN GOD WE TRUST"

Pastor Ray

MARCH 5

KNOW THAT GOD IS WITH YOU

Josh 1:8-9

8 This book of the law shall not depart out of thy mouth; but thou shalt meditate therein day and night, that thou mayest observe to do according to all that is written therein: for then thou shalt make thy way prosperous, and then thou shalt have good success. **9** Have not I commanded thee? Be strong and of a good courage; be not afraid, neither be thou dismayed: for the Lord thy God is with thee whithersoever thou goest. KJV

God wants us to be strong, brave, not afraid, knowing that He is with us. If He be for us who can be against us. Let God have His place in your life. Meditate His word and be a success in all that you set your heart and mind to do.

PRAY AND LET GOD LEAD, HAVE A LOVELY DAY

"IN GOD WE TRUST"

Pastor Ray

MARCH 6

GOD IS YOUR REFUGE

Ps 91:9-13

9 Because thou hast made the Lord, which is my refuge, even the most High, thy habitation; **10** There shall no evil befall thee, neither shall any plague come nigh thy dwelling. **11** For he shall give his angels charge over thee, to keep thee in all thy ways. **12** They shall bear thee up in their hands, lest thou dash thy foot against a stone. **13** Thou shalt tread upon the lion and adder: the young lion and the dragon shalt thou trample under feet. KJV

God has placed you in the care of an army of angels, they are there to protect you from evil and harm, and to help you, but you have to be willing to let them do there job, they will not force you to be protected, you have to allow it to happen.

IN JESUS' NAME, MAKE YOUR NEED KNOWN TO THEM, AND HAVE A GREAT DAY

"IN GOD WE TRUST"

MARCH 7

GODS GIFT TO YOU, FORGIVENESS, AND HEALING

1 Peter 2:23-25

23 Who, when he was reviled, reviled not again; when he suffered, he threatened not; but committed himself to him that judgeth righteously: **24** Who his own self bare our sins in his own body on the tree, that we, being dead to sins, should live unto righteousness: by whose stripes ye were healed. **25** For ye were as sheep going astray; but are now returned unto the Shepherd and Bishop of your souls. KJV

Notice the word were, it is past tense which means that your sins are already forgiven, and you have been healed, it has been bought and paid for by the stripes Jesus took for you and I. Don't let anyone steal from you what is yours, it is a gift given to you. Fight to keep it.

ACCEPT HIS GIFT, AND HAVE A QUITE AND PEACEFUL DAY.

"IN GOD WE TRUST"

MARCH 8

BE OF GOOD COURAGE, GOD WILL KEEP HIS WORD

Rom 4:19-25

19 And being not weak in faith, he considered not his own body now dead, when he was about an hundred years old, neither yet the deadness of Sara's womb: **20** He staggered not at the promise of God through unbelief; but was strong in faith, giving glory to God; **21** And being fully persuaded that, what he had promised, he was able also to perform. **22** And therefore it was imputed to him for righteousness. **23** Now it was not written for his sake alone, that it was imputed to him; **24** But for us also, to whom it shall be imputed, if we believe on him that raised up Jesus our Lord from the dead; **25** Who was delivered for our offences, and was raised again for our justification. KJV

In today's times with all the disregard for human life, we need to know we have someone we can depend on. When the Word of God makes the long 18" journey from our head to our heart and becomes an integral part of our very being, then we will begin to grasp the awesome truth that God really does care and wants nothing but the best for us. Our part is to believe that He is able to perform what he has said He would.

BELIEVE AND RECEIVE, HAVE A GREAT DAY

"IN GOD WE TRUST"

Pastor Ray

MARCH 9

DO NOT LET YOUR HEART BE TROUBLED, EVERYTHING IS GOING TO BE ALL RIGHT

John 14:25-27

25 These things have I spoken unto you, being yet present with you. **26** But the Comforter, which is the Holy Ghost, whom the Father will send in my name, he shall teach you all things, and bring all things to your remembrance, whatsoever I have said unto you. **27** Peace I leave with you, my peace I give unto you: not as the world giveth, give I unto you. Let not your heart be troubled, neither let it be afraid. KJV

This is your promise from God, to give you peace of mind, it is a gift for you from your heavenly Father which only He can give. Our part is to give Him all of our problems, believing that He truly loves us and is able to help us through the situation to a victorious conclusion.

TRUST HIM, AND HAVE A GOOD DAY

"IN GOD WE TRUST"

Pastor Ray

MARCH 10

WATCH YOUR WORDS

Prov 13:1-4

A wise son heareth his father's instruction: but a scorner heareth not rebuke. **2** A man shall eat good by the fruit of his mouth: but the soul of the transgressors shall eat violence. **3** He that keepeth his mouth keepeth his life: but he that openeth wide his lips shall have destruction. **4** The soul of the sluggard desireth, and hath nothing: but the soul of the diligent shall be made fat. KJV

Our words can be helpful or hurtful, we should learn that if we can not say something good and constructive, we should not say anything. With our words we build up or tear down. Our words are constructive and we should use them wisely.

WHAT YOU SAY IS WHAT YOU GET. HAVE A GREAT DAY.

"IN GOD WE TRUST"

Pastor Ray

MARCH 11

HONESTY PAYS GOOD DIVIDENDS

Prov 14:2-3

2 He that walketh in his uprightness feareth the Lord: but he that is perverse in his ways despiseth him. **3** In the mouth of the foolish is a rod of pride: but the lips of the wise shall preserve them. KJV

Being honest with God will cause Him to reward you in ways you could never dream of.

RESPECT GOD AND BE BLESSED, HAVE A GREAT DAY

"IN GOD WE TRUST"

MARCH 12

HOLD YOUR HEAD HIGH

Luke 21:25-28

25 And there shall be signs in the sun, and in the moon, and in the stars; and upon the earth distress of nations, with perplexity; the sea and the waves roaring; **26** Men's hearts failing them for fear, and for looking after those things which are coming on the earth: for the powers of heaven shall be shaken. **27** And then shall they see the Son of man coming in a cloud with power and great glory. **28** And when these things begin to come to pass, then look up, and lift up your heads; for your redemption draweth nigh. KJV

We may ask what things? The day of the vengeance of the Lord. When we see these times we know that we should look up and hold our heads up for our redemption draws neigh. We don't have to wait until the end times, I would much rather go through them with Him than without Him, for God will give us our redemption when we ask. Hold your head up, be not ashamed, you are redeemed when you ask.

ASK AND RECEIVE, HAVE A JOYFUL DAY

"IN GOD WE TRUST"

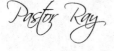

MARCH 13

HIS WAY IS JOY

Job 8:19-22

19 Behold, this is the joy of his way, and out of the earth shall others grow. 20 Behold, God will not cast away a perfect man, neither will he help the evil doers: 21 Till he fill thy mouth with laughing, and thy lips with rejoicing. 22 They that hate thee shall be clothed with shame; and the dwelling place of the wicked shall come to nought. KJV

God cares for those who love him, He will let his joy fill you, put your enemies to shame and bring you out on top with joy and laughter in your heart, and your lips singing praise to Him as you rejoice in His presence.

LET HIS JOY FILL YOUR DAY, AND HAVE A GOOD ONE.

"IN GOD WE TRUST"

MARCH 14

THE JOY OF THE LORD IS YOUR STRENGTH

Nehemiah 8:10

10 Then he said unto them, Go your way, eat the fat, and drink the sweet, and send portions unto them for whom nothing is prepared: for this day is holy unto our Lord: neither be ye sorry; for the joy of the LORD is your strength. KJV

We are encouraged not to feel sorry for ourselves or be sad, but to celebrate with a feast of choice foods and sweet drinks (maybe a pot luck) and share with those who have nothing prepared, invite someone and tell them to bring nothing but themselves, for God gives us joy when we help others, and His joy is our strength.

PRAISE HIM, FOR IT GIVES HIM JOY

"IN GOD WE TRUST"

Pastor Ray

MARCH 15

YOU CAN HAVE FULLNESS OF JOY

Ps 16:8-11

8 I have set the Lord always before me: because he is at my right hand, I shall not be moved. **9** Therefore my heart is glad, and my glory rejoiceth: my flesh also shall rest in hope. **10** For thou wilt not leave my soul in hell; neither wilt thou suffer thine Holy One to see corruption. **11** Thou wilt shew me the path of life: in thy presence is fulness of joy; at thy right hand there are pleasures for evermore. KJV

This is the position God wants us to be in, close to Him, in His presence, so we can have fullness of joy and pleasure for evermore. He is our Father God and wishes to share our joy and pleasure, as our fullness of joy gives Him great pleasure.

LET HIM SHOW THE WAY, AND HAVE A GREAT AND JOY FILLED LIFE

"IN GOD WE TRUST"

MARCH 16

DON'T KNOW WHICH WAY TO TURN?

Prov 3:5-8

5 Trust in the Lord with all thine heart; and lean not unto thine own understanding. **6** In all thy ways acknowledge him, and he shall direct thy paths. **7** Be not wise in thine own eyes: fear the Lord, and depart from evil. **8** It shall be health to thy navel, and marrow to thy bones. KJV

Our problem is that most of the time we are the ones deciding which way to go and then want God to make the way easy. If we will only learn to trust Him, then hear where He wants us to go. We ask for directions, then go the opposite of what he tells us, He says go right at the fork in the road because He knows the bridge is out on the left road, but no we go left because we know it is the shortest way not knowing the bridge is out and that we will have to come all the way back and then take the right road, then gripe because it took to long.

PRAY, LISTEN, AND ACT ON WHAT YOU HEAR FROM GOD. HAVE A PROSPEROUS AND HAPPY DAY.

"IN GOD WE TRUST"

MARCH 17

DON'T GIVE UP

Rev 3:20-21

20 Behold, I stand at the door, and knock: if any man hear my voice, and open the door, I will come in to him, and will sup with him, and he with me. **21** To him that overcometh will I grant to sit with me in my throne, even as I also overcame, and am set down with my Father in his throne. KJV

This is a promise to everyone, if we will hang in there, and trust God, as He has also promised never to leave us or forsake us. Keep your faith and trust God to bring us through to the victory.

STAY ON THE WINNING SIDE, AND HAVE A GREAT DAY

"IN GOD WE TRUST"

Pastor Ray

MARCH 18

YOUR WORD ARE PRODUCTIVE

Prov 21:23-24

23 Whoever guards his mouth and tongue Keeps his soul from troubles. **24** A proud *and* haughty *man*—"Scoffer" *is* his name; He acts with arrogant pride. NKJV

In the beginning God created everything with His words. (example Gen 1:3-5 3 And God said, "Let there be light," and there was light. 4 God saw that the light was good, and he separated the light from the darkness. 5 God called the light "day," and the darkness he called "night." And there was evening, and there was morning—the first day.) Let us all remember that we are created in His image, therefore our words are productive.

WHAT YOU SAY IS WHAT YOU GET.

"IN GOD WE TRUST"

Pastor Ray

MARCH 19

LET GOD BE YOUR GUIDE

Prov 22:26-28

26 Be not thou one of them that strike hands, or of them that are sureties for debts. **27** If thou hast nothing to pay, why should he take away thy bed from under thee? **28** Remove not the ancient landmark, which thy fathers have set. KJV

Stay close to God for He will make something good out of something bad, He knows what the end of things will be, so let us pray, and wait patently for the Lord to act. (2 Chron 7:14 If my people, which are called by my name, shall humble themselves, and pray, and seek my face, and turn from their wicked ways; then will I hear from heaven, and will forgive their sin, and will heal their land. KJV)

STAY YOUR COURSE, HOLD ONTO GOD, AND HAVE A GOOD DAY.

"IN GOD WE TRUST"

MARCH 20

GOD SHALL SUPPLY YOUR NEED

Phil 4:18-20

18 But I have all, and abound: I am full, having received of Epaphroditus the things which were sent from you, an odour of a sweet smell, a sacrifice acceptable, wellpleasing to God. **19** But my God shall supply all your need according to his riches in glory by Christ Jesus. **20** Now unto God and our Father be glory for ever and ever. Amen. KJV

Notice that the scripture says all of your need. God knows us better than we know ourselves, He knows all of our needs and will meet them when we decide to receive and get our selves into the right position with Him, by accepting Jesus as our Lord and savior and believing that He is the Son of God. When we are in right standing with Him He will meet our need as it arises, one at a time.

BE BLESSED, AND HAVE A NICE DAY

"IN GOD WE TRUST"

Pastor Ray

MARCH 21

YOU HAVE A FUTURE

Jer 29:8-11

8 For thus saith the Lord of hosts, the God of Israel; Let not your prophets and your diviners, that be in the midst of you, deceive you, neither hearken to your dreams which ye cause to be dreamed. **9** For they prophesy falsely unto you in my name: I have not sent them, saith the Lord. **10** For thus saith the Lord, That after seventy years be accomplished at Babylon I will visit you, and perform my good word toward you, in causing you to return to this place. **11** For I know the thoughts that I think toward you, saith the Lord, thoughts of peace, and not of evil, to give you an expected end. KJV

Your future is secure, for God knows the plans He has for you, as He shows His love toward us in many ways. The more we yield to Him the easier it is for Him to fulfill those plans, plans for good things, not bad. So keep your hopes alive for your future is secure.

LET GOD HAVE HIS WAY, AND ENJOY YOUR DAY.

"IN GOD WE TRUST"

Pastor Ray

MARCH 22

YOU ARE VERY SPECIAL

Zeph 3:16-17

16 In that day it shall be said to Jerusalem, Fear thou not: and to Zion, Let not thine hands be slack. **17** The Lord thy God in the midst of thee is mighty; he will save, he will rejoice over thee with joy; he will rest in his love, he will joy over thee with singing. KJV

Put your name in the place of Jerusalem and Zion, then receive these scriptures as a personal note to you from God, and know that He has always loved you, even when you thought He did not know you existed. His heart is saddened when we get out from under His umbrella of protection, but He rejoices when we come back home to Him. The desire of Gods heart is to love and protect you, but you have to allow Him to do so as He will not force to do anything.

LET GO AND LET GOD. HAVE A GREAT DAY, AND A JOYFUL WEEKEND.

"IN GOD WE TRUST"

MARCH 23

MENDING RELATIONSHIPS

Matt 7:7-12

7 Ask, and it shall be given you; seek, and ye shall find; knock, and it shall be opened unto you: **8** For every one that asketh receiveth; and he that seeketh findeth; and to him that knocketh it shall be opened. **9** Or what man is there of you, whom if his son ask bread, will he give him a stone? **10** Or if he ask a fish, will he give him a serpent? **11** If ye then, being evil, know how to give good gifts unto your children, how much more shall your Father which is in heaven give good things to them that ask him? **12** Therefore all things whatsoever ye would that men should do to you, do ye even so to them: for this is the law and the prophets. KJV

If you have a problem with any relationship these scriptures give you the answer to getting it taken care of. If you can only bring yourself to being kind to someone who is being ugly to You. Loving someone who you think hates us, then you are getting close to healing the relationship with Gods love.

ASK AND RECEIVE. HAVE A GREAT DAY.

"IN GOD WE TRUST"

Pastor Ray

MARCH 24

LET GO AND LET GOD

Matt 5:43-48

43 Ye have heard that it hath been said, Thou shalt love thy neighbour, and hate thine enemy. **44** But I say unto you, Love your enemies, bless them that curse you, do good to them that hate you, and pray for them which despitefully use you, and persecute you; **45** That ye may be the children of your Father which is in heaven: for he maketh his sun to rise on the evil and on the good, and sendeth rain on the just and on the unjust. **46** For if ye love them which love you, what reward have ye? do not even the publicans the same? **47** And if ye salute your brethren only, what do ye more than others? do not even the publicans so? **48** Be ye therefore perfect, even as your Father which is in heaven is perfect. KJV

If you will let go and pray for those who mistreat you and let God handle it, as He can do a much better job than you or I can, then His peace which passes all understanding will flood over you, as you realize that God loves you and is more than able to take care of your problems.

LET GO AND LET GOD GIVE YOU A GREAT WEEK END

"IN GOD WE TRUST"

Pastor Ray

MARCH 25

YOU ARE FORGIVEN

Ephesians 4:29-32

29 Let no corrupt communication proceed out of your mouth, but that which is good to the use of edifying, that it may minister grace unto the hearers. 30 And grieve not the holy Spirit of God, whereby ye are sealed unto the day of redemption. 31 Let all bitterness, and wrath, and anger, and clamour, and evil speaking, be put away from you, with all malice: 32 And be ye kind one to another, tenderhearted, forgiving one another, even as God for Christ's sake hath forgiven you. KJV

Unforgiveness will cause anger to be present in your heart, and out of the abundance of the heart your mouth speaks. Again let go and let God, forgive for you are forgiven. Notice the word hath which is past tense, which means it is already done.

YOU ARE FORGIVEN. HAVE A GREAT DAY

"IN GOD WE TRUST"

Pastor Ray

MARCH 26

KEEP YOUR VISION SHARP

Prov 29:18

18 Where there is no vision, the people perish: but he that keepeth the law, happy is he. KJV

Let us all keep our vision sharp and on Gods ways so that we do not stumble and fall, when we follow Gods ways we invite His blessings to overtake us.

SLOW DOWN, AND LET HIS BLESSINGS CATCH YOU. HAVE A NICE DAY.

"IN GOD WE TRUST"

Pastor Ray

MARCH 27

GODS COVENANT PROMISE, THE POWER TO GET WEALTH, IS FOR YOU

Deut 8:17-18

17 And thou say in thine heart, My power and the might of mine hand hath gotten me this wealth. **18** But thou shalt remember the Lord thy God: for it is he that giveth thee power to get wealth, that he may establish his covenant which he sware unto thy fathers, as it is this day. KJV

With a promise like this how can we begin to think that God does not want us to be prosperous in every area of our life. Even though the covenant was made with our ancestors, it is for us this day, so receive the power to get wealth and put it to work in your life. It is your heritage, but remember who gave it to you, and why. The purpose of this gift is to establish His covenant with you.

HE IS A COVENANT KEEPING GOD. STAY WITH HIM AND HAVE A NICE DAY.

"IN GOD WE TRUST"

MARCH 28

GODS GIFTS TO YOU, HEALING

1 Peter 2:21-25

21 For even hereunto were ye called: because Christ also suffered for us, leaving us an example, that ye should follow his steps: **22** Who did no sin, neither was guile found in his mouth: **23** Who, when he was reviled, reviled not again; when he suffered, he threatened not; but committed himself to him that judgeth righteously: **24** Who his own self bare our sins in his own body on the tree, that we, being dead to sins, should live unto righteousness: by whose stripes ye were healed. **25** For ye were as sheep going astray; but are now returned unto the Shepherd and Bishop of your souls. KJV

Notice the words "ye were", they are past tense which means that you already have been healed and health is yours. Don't let anyone steal from you what is yours, Jesus paid an awesome price for healing and has given it to you. Fight to keep it. It is like having money in the bank and refusing to write a check when you are hungry and don't have the cash on hand to buy food.

RECEIVE HIS GIFT, AND HAVE A DAY

"IN GOD WE TRUST"

Pastor Ray

MARCH 29

FEAR IS NOT FOR YOU

2 Tim 1:7-10

7 For God hath not given us the spirit of fear; but of power, and of love, and of a sound mind. **8** Be not thou therefore ashamed of the testimony of our Lord, nor of me his prisoner: but be thou partaker of the afflictions of the gospel according to the power of God; **9** Who hath saved us, and called us with an holy calling, not according to our works, but according to his own purpose and grace, which was given us in Christ Jesus before the world began, **10** But is now made manifest by the appearing of our Saviour Jesus Christ, who hath abolished death, and hath brought life and immortality to light through the gospel: KJV

When fear knocks at your door, let your faith answer and there will be no one there. Your gift from God is power, love and a sound mind,

NOT FEAR. DON'T BE FOOLED, HAVE A GOOD DAY.

"IN GOD WE TRUST"

Pastor Ray

MARCH 30

YOUR ANGER IS HARMFUL

James 1:19-21

19 Wherefore, my beloved brethren, let every man be swift to hear, slow to speak, slow to wrath: **20** For the wrath of man worketh not the righteousness of God. **21** Wherefore lay apart all filthiness and superfluity of naughtiness, and receive with meekness the engrafted word, which is able to save your souls. KJV

Anger is first of all harmful to you, and then to all around you, It will destroy relationships and cause you great sorrow for the words you have spoken. Determine in your heart not to let the sun go down on your wrath. My wife and I made that decision many years ago, and we believe it has played a big part in our marriage lasting sixty two beautiful years before she went to be with the Lord. We decided to not go to sleep angry at each other, oh there were a few long nights mostly in the first two years, but not many, and none since then.

BE KIND TO EACH OTHER IN EVERY RELATIONSHIP, AND HAVE A GREAT DAY.

"IN GOD WE TRUST"

Pastor Ray

MARCH 31

DON'T LOSE HOPE

Prov 13:11-12

11 Wealth gotten by vanity shall be diminished: but he that gathereth by labour shall increase. **12** Hope deferred maketh the heart sick: but when the desire cometh, it is a tree of life. KJV

Easy come easy go blurs your vision and dims your hope, your hope is the blue print of what you are believing for, and when we begin to lose our hope it is like a blue print when the lines have started to fade and you are no longer able to make out the desired object. It is like when our vision is blurred, we are hoping for something we do not have a clear picture of inside of us. DON'T LOSE YOUR HOPE, KEEP YOUR VISION SHARP UNTIL YOU HAVE RECEIVED WHAT YOU ARE HOPING FOR

THEN LET YOUR JOY OVERFLOW. AND HAVE A HAPPY EASTER.

"IN GOD WE TRUST"

Pastor Ray

APRIL 1

A MERRY HEART IS LIKE A MEDICINE

Prov 15:11-13

11 Hell and destruction are before the Lord: how much more then the hearts of the children of men? **12** A scorner loveth not one that reproveth him: neither will he go unto the wise. **13** A merry heart maketh a cheerful countenance: but by sorrow of the heart the spirit is broken. KJV

A merry heart acts like a medicine for you. Don't let worry, sorrow, and sadness overtake you, determine that you are going to be glad and rejoice, even when you don't feel like it, for the joy of the Lord is your strength, it brings a smile to your face, and joy in your heart, and prosperity in every area of your life.

LAUGH AND THE WORLD LAUGHS WITH YOU.

"IN GOD WE TRUST"

APRIL 2

HOW TO STAY OUT OF TROUBLE

Prov 5:1-2

My son, attend unto my wisdom, and bow thine ear to my understanding: **2** That thou mayest regard discretion, and that thy lips may keep knowledge. KJV

Listen to God, hear what He tells you, and be quick to obey, delayed obedience and long consideration will cause you to miss out on what God is trying to do for you. If you don't act on His word, He will find someone else who will.

HEAR AND OBEY, AND HAVE A GREAT DAY.

"IN GOD WE TRUST"

APRIL 3

HURTING? RUN TO GOD

Proverbs 18:10

10 The name of the LORD is a strong tower: the righteous runneth into it, and is safe.

The King James Version, (Cambridge: Cambridge) 1769.

God always has his arm outstretched for us to run into, He loves to be able to put His arms around us and comfort us when we need help, no matter what the problem may be. God is our loving heavenly Father, we should always run to Him and not away from Him, as He is always there waiting for us to make the move towards Him.

MAKE YOUR MOVE, AND HAVE A GREAT DAY.

"IN GOD WE TRUST"

Pastor Ray

APRIL 4

GOD WANTS YOU TO HAVE A GOOD LIFE

Prov 21:21-23

21 He that followeth after righteousness and mercy findeth life, righteousness, and honour. **22** A wise man scaleth the city of the mighty, and casteth down the strength of the confidence thereof. **23** Whoso keepeth his mouth and his tongue keepeth his soul from troubles. KJV

We are told in Proverbs 3:1-2 that if we keep His commandments we will have a long life worth living, that means with peace, Love, righteousness, and honor, finding favor with God and man. We are created in Gods image and our words are productive, don't speak what you do not want.

WHAT YOU SAY IS WHAT YOU GET, SAY GOOD THINGS AND HAVE A GREAT DAY.

"IN GOD WE TRUST"

APRIL 5

YOU ARE CHOSEN OF GOD TO BE HIS TEMPLE

1 Cor 6:18-20

committeth fornication sinneth against his own body. **19** What? know ye not that your body is the temple of the Holy Ghost which is in you, which ye have of God, and ye are not your own? **20** For ye are bought with a price: therefore glorify God in your body, and in your spirit, which are God's. KJV

The Holy Spirit of God has been given to you, to give you power to be a witness for Him, also to give you power to go through every situation you are faced with, to give you strength to overcome, to make you the head and not the tail, to place you above and not beneath, to make you a temple suitable for Him to reside in throughout eternity. If you have not already done so, Let today be the time of establishment of that temple

HAVE A BLESSED AND HAPPY DAY

"IN GOD WE TRUST"

Pastor Ray

APRIL 6

YOU ARE A VERY SPECIAL PERSON

John 15:11-15

11 These things have I spoken unto you, that my joy might remain in you, and that your joy might be full. **12** This is my commandment, That ye love one another, as I have loved you. **13** Greater love hath no man than this, that a man lay down his life for his friends. **14** Ye are my friends, if ye do whatsoever I command you. **15** Henceforth I call you not servants; for the servant knoweth not what his lord doeth: but I have called you friends; for all things that I have heard of my Father I have made known unto you.

KJV

You are very special to God, He picked you out of the crowd to be His, so that He could love you, and share with you He has made you His friend, and trusts you enough to have the fruit of His Spirit produced in abundance in your life, then whatever we ask for in the name of Jesus, He can trust us enough to give it to us.

BE A FRIEND OF JESUS, AND HAVE A LOVELY DAY.

"IN GOD WE TRUST"

APRIL 7

YOU HAVE OVERCOME

1 John 4:4-6

4 Ye are of God, little children, and have overcome them: because greater is he that is in you, than he that is in the world. **5** They are of the world: therefore speak they of the world, and the world heareth them. **6** We are of God: he that knoweth God heareth us; he that is not of God heareth not us. Hereby know we the spirit of truth, and the spirit of error. KJV

You are a child of God if you have accepted the Lord Jesus as your savor, thus you are an overcomer, and have been translated into the kingdom of Gods dear Son, notice the word have, which is past tense, which means it has been done already, because the Lord Jesus Christ, the anointed, the greater one is resident in you, which gives you the victory.

YOU HAVE OVERCOME BECAUSE HE IS RISEN.

"IN GOD WE TRUST"

Pastor Ray

APRIL 8

GOD IS WATCHING OVER YOU

Ps 11:4-6

4 The Lord is in his holy temple, the Lord's throne is in heaven: his eyes behold, his eyelids try, the children of men. **5** The Lord trieth the righteous: but the wicked and him that loveth violence his soul hateth. **6** Upon the wicked he shall rain snares, fire and brimstone, and an horrible tempest: this shall be the portion of their cup. KJV

God sees everything, when we sin He is there, when we repent of sin He is there, He sees when we are good and when we are bad. God is no respecter of persons, we will get what we deserve, good or bad. His love is what He wants to give us, but He will not force it on us, so do good and receive His blessings. Deut 30:19 tells us "I call heaven and earth to record this day against you, that I have set before you life and death, blessing and cursing: therefore choose life, that both thou and thy seed may live: KJV"

THE CHOICE IS OURS.

"IN GOD WE TRUST"

Pastor Ray

APRIL 9

GODS LOVE WILL SEE YOU THROUGH

Romans 5:1-5

Therefore being justified by faith, we have peace with God through our Lord Jesus Christ: 2 By whom also we have access by faith into this grace wherein we stand, and rejoice in hope of the glory of God. 3 And not only so, but we glory in tribulations also: knowing that tribulation worketh patience; 4 And patience, experience; and experience, hope: 5 And hope maketh not ashamed; because the love of God is shed abroad in our hearts by the Holy Ghost which is given unto us.

The King James Version, (Cambridge: Cambridge) 1769.

Gods love is stronger than any trial or tribulation we can face He does not cause them, but uses them to develop our faith and teach us patience, which make us victorious over the situation, which wipes away any shame we may have in the matter. Our anger or bitterness over the situation will drive people from us and Him, but His love flowing through us to those around us will draw them to us and Him.

RECEIVE HIS LOVE, AND HAVE A GREAT AND PROSPEROUS DAY

"IN GOD WE TRUST"

Pastor Ray

APRIL 10

GOD HAS CHOSEN YOU

1 Cor 6:18-20

18 Flee fornication. Every sin that a man doeth is without the body; but he that committeth fornication sinneth against his own body. **19** What? know ye not that your body is the temple of the Holy Ghost which is in you, which ye have of God, and ye are not your own? **20** For ye are bought with a price: therefore glorify God in your body, and in your spirit, which are God's. KJV

The Holy Spirit of God has been given to you to give you power to be a witness for Him, also to give you power to go through every situation and temptation that you are faced with, to give you a way out, and the strength to overcome, to make you the head and not the tail, to place you above and not beneath,

YOUR ARE A CHOSEN ONE, HAVE A GREAT DAY

"IN GOD WE TRUST"

April 11

GOD IS WITH YOU

Deuteronomy 31:6

6 Be strong and of a good courage, fear not, nor be afraid of them: for the LORD thy God, he it is that doth go with thee; he will not fail thee, nor forsake thee.

The King James Version, (Cambridge: Cambridge) 1769.

God is not only with you, He goes out ahead of you to prepare the way that you will find favor. Don't let fear steal your victory. Even when we think He is nowhere around, He is there, He promised that He would not fail you or forsake you, and God keeps His promises. His word is true and it works in our lives.

LET GOD HAVE HIS WAY. HAVE A GREAT DAY.

"IN GOD WE TRUST"

APRIL 12

GOD WANTS YOU WELL ADVISED, AND SAFE

Prov 15:1-3

A soft answer turneth away wrath: but grievous words stir up anger. **2** The tongue of the wise useth knowledge aright: but the mouth of fools poureth out foolishness. **3** The eyes of the Lord are in every place, beholding the evil and the good. KJV

God not only wants you to have wise council and live in safety, but our nations as well. Join me in prayer that we will be blessed with wise and Godly leadership in our nations, states, cites, homes, and Churches.

"IN GOD WE TRUST"

Pastor Ray

APRIL 13

GOD HAS YOU ON HIS MIND

Prov 16:1-3

The preparations of the heart in man, and the answer of the tongue, is from the Lord. **2** All the ways of a man are clean in his own eyes; but the Lord weigheth the spirits. **3** Commit thy works unto the Lord, and thy thoughts shall be established. KJV

Don't accept just anything, become a partner with God, and let Him be your pilot, and you be the co pilot, not only will your thoughts be established, but you plans will be successful, and your way will be straight.

GIVE GOD THE CONTROLS, AND SET BACK AND RELAX. HAVE A GREAT DAY.

"IN GOD WE TRUST"

APRIL 14

BELIEVING IS RECEIVING

John 15:5-8

5 I am the vine, ye are the branches: He that abideth in me, and I in him, the same bringeth forth much fruit: for without me ye can do nothing. **6** If a man abide not in me, he is cast forth as a branch, and is withered; and men gather them, and cast them into the fire, and they are burned. **7** If ye abide in me, and my words abide in you, ye shall ask what ye will, and it shall be done unto you. **8** Herein is my Father glorified, that ye bear much fruit; so shall ye be my disciples. KJV

When we put God and His Word first place in our lives, and truly believe what He says in His word, then we will receive because we believe. Fill yourself with His Word, stay hooked up to Him, this is the way we abide in Him, and by being full of His Word He abides in us.

BELIEVE, AND RECEIVE HIS BLESSINGS. HAVE A GREAT DAY.

"IN GOD WE TRUST"

Pastor Ray

APRIL 15

YOU ARE MORE THAN CONQUERS

Prov 18:14-16

14 The spirit of a man will sustain his infirmity; but a wounded spirit who can bear? **15** The heart of the prudent getteth knowledge; and the ear of the wise seeketh knowledge. **16** A man's gift maketh room for him, and bringeth him before great men. KJV

A wise person will allow God's love to engulf them and keep them wise, healthy, and strong. God's love for you will always keep His arms out stretched for you to come into for protection. With God on your side you are more than conquers.

LET GOD LEAD YOU. HAVE A GREAT DAY

"IN GOD WE TRUST"

Pastor Ray

APRIL 16

GOD WILL LEAD YOU IN THE PATH OF RIGHTEOUSNESS

Prov 19:1-3

Better is the poor that walketh in his integrity, than he that is perverse in his lips, and is a fool. **2** Also, that the soul be without knowledge, it is not good; and he that hasteth with his feet sinneth. **3** The foolishness of man perverteth his way: and his heart fretteth against the Lord. KJV

God wants us to be healthy and wise. He wants for us to speak words of encouragement to those we speak with, and do unto others as we wish for them to do to us. In other words His desire for us is to put our minds in gear before we open our mouths, It is very easy to listen to a lot of chatter about other people and then join in the ripping them apart. If we cant say anything good, then we should say nothing, let the Holy Spirit of God lead us to exhort, edify, and comfort, especially those of our own household.

GUARD YOUR TONGUE, WALK WITH GOD, AND HAVE A NICE DAY

"IN GOD WE TRUST"

APRIL 17

DO NOT BE DECEIVED

Prov 20:1-3

Wine is a mocker, strong drink is raging: and whosoever is deceived thereby is not wise. **2** The fear of a king is as the roaring of a lion: whoso provoketh him to anger sinneth against his own soul. **3** It is an honour for a man to cease from strife: but every fool will be meddling. KJV

Prov 20:1-3

1 WINE IS a mocker, strong drink a riotous brawler; and whoever errs *or* reels because of it is not wise. [Prov 23:29,30; Isa 28:7; Hos 4:11.] **2** The terror of a king is as the roaring of a lion; whoever provokes him to anger *or* angers himself against him sins against his own life. **3** It is an honor for a man to cease from strife *and* keep aloof from it, but every fool will quarrel. AMP

It takes a bigger and better person to walk away from a fight, and to say no when you are tempted with drugs, whether it be alcohol, something you take, or smoke. do not be deceived that kind of joy is short lived, but the joy of the Lord lasts forever.

BE BLESSED AND TAKE CARE OF YOURSELF. HAVE A GREAT DAY.

"IN GOD WE TRUST"

Pastor Ray

APRIL 18

BE PREPARED

2 Tim 2:20-21

But in a great house there are not only vessels of gold and of silver, but also of wood and of earth; and some to honour, and some to dishonour. **21** If a man therefore purge himself from these, he shall be a vessel unto honour, sanctified, and meet for the master's use, and prepared unto every good work. KJV

God wants us to be vessels suited to contain the triune God Head, God the Father, God the Son, and God the Holy Spirit, and prepared for every good work. Prepared in season and out of season to share His Words with those who may not have heard them. God wants us to share His word in love, not to try to ram it down their throat. Let His love flow through you to others.

BE PREPARED AS A VESSEL OF HONOUR. HAVE A GREAT DAY

"IN GOD WE TRUST"

Pastor Ray

APRIL 19

GOD'S WISDOM IS FOR YOU

Prov 22:17-21

17 Bow down thine ear, and hear the words of the wise, and apply thine heart unto my knowledge. **18** For it is a pleasant thing if thou keep them within thee; they shall withal be fitted in thy lips. **19** That thy trust may be in the Lord, I have made known to thee this day, even to thee. **20** Have not I written to thee excellent things in counsels and knowledge, **21** That I might make thee know the certainty of the words of truth; that thou mightest answer the words of truth to them that send unto thee? KJV

You are special to God, He wants you to be smart and healthy, wealthy and wise, He has it all planned out for you to take and run with it, God wants you to share His Word with all that have ears to hear.

RECEIVE GOD'S BLESSINGS, AND HAVE A GOOD DAY

"IN GOD WE TRUST"

Pastor Ray

APRIL 20

YOU HAVE HELP WITH ALL YOUR CARES

1 Peter 5:6-8

6 Humble yourselves therefore under the mighty hand of God, that he may exalt you in due time: **7** Casting all your care upon him; for he careth for you. **8** Be sober, be vigilant; because your adversary the devil, as a roaring lion, walketh about, seeking whom he may devour: KJV

Let God help you through your trials and troubles, go to Him in prayer making your need known to Him, then leave them there with Him, for He loves you and cares for you. Jesus paid the price we could not pay for all our iniquities and sin so we don't have to try to carry them any further.

KEEP YOUR GUARD UP. HAVE A NICE DAY

"IN GOD WE TRUST"

APRIL 21

GOD IS ON YOUR SIDE

Rom 8:31-35

31 What shall we then say to these things? If God be for us, who can be against us? **32** He that spared not his own Son, but delivered him up for us all, how shall he not with him also freely give us all things? **33** Who shall lay any thing to the charge of God's elect? It is God that justifieth. **34** Who is he that condemneth? It is Christ that died, yea rather, that is risen again, who is even at the right hand of God, who also maketh intercession for us. **35** Who shall separate us from the love of Christ? shall tribulation, or distress, or persecution, or famine, or nakedness, or peril, or sword? KJV

When God is for us we have an army of His angels around us to see that we are protected. Our part is to rest assured that God means what He says, have faith in Him, and know that He is able to stand behind His Word to perform it. He put every thing on the line for us, and He will protect His investment.

THE LEAST WE CAN DO IS SURRENDER TO HIM. HAVE A GOOD DAY

"IN GOD WE TRUST"

APRIL 22

GOD'S PROMISES ARE HIS GIFTS TO YOU

2 Cor 1:20-22

20 For all the promises of God in him are yea, and in him Amen, unto the glory of God by us. **21** Now he which stablisheth us with you in Christ, and hath anointed us, is God; **22** Who hath also sealed us, and given the earnest of the Spirit in our hearts. KJV

2 Cor 1:20-22

20 For no matter how many promises God has made, they are "Yes" in Christ. And so through him the "Amen" is spoken by us to the glory of God. **21** Now it is God who makes both us and you stand firm in Christ. He anointed us, **22** set his seal of ownership on us, and put his Spirit in our hearts as a deposit, guaranteeing what is to come. NIV

God never makes a promise that He does not keep, and what He gives He will not take away from us. He has given us the measure of faith with which we can believe Him for what His word says, and believe His promises are true and for us today. Beloved (that's you) I wish for you to prosper and be in good health

TRUST HIM, HE LOVES US TO MUCH TO LEAVE US THE WAY WE ARE. HAVE A GOOD SUNDAY, AND A GREAT WEEK

"IN GOD WE TRUST"

APRIL 23

YOUR NEED IS MET

Phil 4:19-20

19 But my God shall supply all your need according to his riches in glory by Christ Jesus. **20** Now unto God and our Father be glory for ever and ever. Amen. KJV

God is faithful to keep His word, and His Word says that my God shall supply all your need, that's right my God, the God I serve has promised according to his Word to supply all your need according to His riches in glory by Christ Jesus, and God is not one who lies. He also promised where two are agreed on earth as touching anything they shall ask that it would be done for them (Mat 18:19) So let us get in agreement as touching our needs and the needs of our nation that they shall be met by our Father Which is in Heaven, whether they are physical, financial or Spiritual. Also to have a shield of protection around our troops and allies around the world.

AMEN, SO BE IT. HAVE A NICE DAY

"IN GOD WE TRUST"

Pastor Ray

APRIL 24

GOD WILL PROTECT YOU

Ps 27:1-5

The Lord is my light and my salvation; whom shall I fear? the Lord is the strength of my life; of whom shall I be afraid? **2** When the wicked, even mine enemies and my foes, came upon me to eat up my flesh, they stumbled and fell. **3** Though an host should encamp against me, my heart shall not fear: though war should rise against me, in this will I be confident. **4** One thing have I desired of the Lord, that will I seek after; that I may dwell in the house of the Lord all the days of my life, to behold the beauty of the Lord, and to inquire in his temple. **5** For in the time of trouble he shall hide me in his pavilion: in the secret of his tabernacle shall he hide me; he shall set me up upon a rock. KJV

When you walk with God on your side, you can rest assured that you need not be afraid of anything, so enter into that place of quite rest and slam the door shut in the enemies face.

LET GO AND LET GOD, HAVE A FEARLESS DAY.

"IN GOD WE TRUST"

Pastor Ray

APRIL 25

YOU ARE NEVER ALONE

Hag 2:4-5

4 Yet now be strong, O Zerubbabel, saith the Lord; and be strong, O Joshua, son of Josedech, the high priest; and be strong, all ye people of the land, saith the Lord, and work: for I am with you, saith the Lord of hosts: **5** According to the word that I covenanted with you when ye came out of Egypt, so my spirit remaineth among you: fear ye not. KJV

This is for you today, your name may not be Zerubbabel, or Joshua, but you can put your name in there or just be one of the people of the land. His Word is just as true to us today as it was then, He also promised He would never leave us or forsake us, so we can rest assured that He is with us wherever we go and whatever we do. Rest assured that He will bring us through this time with VICTORY.

PUT YOUR TRUST IN GOD, HAVE A GREAT DAY

"IN GOD WE TRUST"

Pastor Ray

APRIL 26

THE PEACE OF GOD IS FOR YOU

Ps 29:10-11

10 The Lord sitteth upon the flood; yea, the Lord sitteth King for ever. **11** The Lord will give strength unto his people; the Lord will bless his people with peace. KJV

Peace is only one of the gifts that God gives to those that love Him, but it is a powerful one that most people desire, peace in their homes, peace in their work places, peace in their neighborhoods, towns, and nation.

ONLY GOD CAN GIVE A LASTING PEACE, RECEIVE IT AND HAVE A GOOD DAY.

"IN GOD WE TRUST"

APRIL 27

GOD HAS CHOSEN YOU

1 Cor 6:17-20

17 But he that is joined unto the Lord is one spirit. **18** Flee fornication. Every sin that a man doeth is without the body; but he that committeth fornication sinneth against his own body. **19** What? know ye not that your body is the temple of the Holy Ghost which is in you, which ye have of God, and ye are not your own? **20** For ye are bought with a price: therefore glorify God in your body, and in your spirit, which are God's. KJV

The Holy Spirit of God has been given to you to give you power to be a witness for Him, and stay out of trouble, also to give you power to go through every situation you are faced with, to give you strength to overcome, to give you a way out, to make you the head and not the tail, to place you above and not beneath.

LET GOD HAVE WHAT IS HIS, "YOU." AND HAVE A GREAT DAY.

"IN GOD WE TRUST"

Pastor Ray

APRIL 28

YOU ARE A VERY SPECIAL PERSON

John 15:16-17

16 Ye have not chosen me, but I have chosen you, and ordained you, that ye should go and bring forth fruit, and that your fruit should remain: that whatsoever ye shall ask of the Father in my name, he may give it you. **17** These things I command you, that ye love one another. KJV

You are very special to God, He picked you out of the crowd to be His, so that He could love you, and have the fruit of His spirit produced in abundance in your life, then whatever you ask for in the name of Jesus, He can trust you enough to give it to you. Why? because you are producing the fruit of His Spirit that remains, love, joy, peace, longsuffering, gentleness, goodness, faith, meekness, temperance: against such there is no law.

YOU ARE CHOSEN OF GOD, HAVE A NICE DAY.

"IN GOD WE TRUST"

Pastor Ray

APRIL 29

YOU HAVE OVERCOME

1 John 4:4-6

4 Ye are of God, little children, and have overcome them: because greater is he that is in you, than he that is in the world. **5** They are of the world: therefore speak they of the world, and the world heareth them. **6** We are of God: he that knoweth God heareth us; he that is not of God heareth not us. Hereby know we the spirit of truth, and the spirit of error. KJV

You are a child of God if you have accepted the Lord Jesus as your savor, thus you are an overcomer, notice the word have, which is past tense, which means it has been done already, because the Lord Jesus Christ the anointed, the greater one is resident in you.

ENJOY YOUR VICTORY, HAVE A GREAT DAY.

"IN GOD WE TRUST"

Pastor Ray

APRIL 30

FEAR NOT, GOD IS WITH YOU

Isa 41:10

10 Fear thou not; for I am with thee: be not dismayed; for I am thy God: I will strengthen thee; yea, I will help thee; yea, I will uphold thee with the right hand of my righteousness. KJV

This promise from God is for you today and forever, He is with you to give you courage to handle every adversity, to keep you going when your to tired to fight, His love for you is unconditional,

LET GOD'S LOVE KEEP YOU SAFE, HAVE A GREAT DAY.

"IN GOD WE TRUST"

Pastor Ray

MAY 1

ARE YOU LOOKING FOR PEACE?

Phil 4:4-7

4 Rejoice in the Lord alway: and again I say, Rejoice. **5** Let your moderation be known unto all men. The Lord is at hand. **6** Be careful for nothing; but in every thing by prayer and supplication with thanksgiving let your requests be made known unto God. **7** And the peace of God, which passeth all understanding, shall keep your hearts and minds through Christ Jesus. KJV

God has already made provisions for us to have His peace. Our part is to go to Him in prayer with thanksgiving in our hearts, and faith in Him that He is able and willing to grant our request. He loves you as a father, for He has chosen you to be in His family. Children translated into the kingdom of His dear Son, and wants you to be blessed in all things.

REJOICE, AND HAVE A HAPPY DAY.

"IN GOD WE TRUST"

MAY 2

ANGER IS HARMFUL

James 1:17-20

17 Every good gift and every perfect gift is from above, and cometh down from the Father of lights, with whom is no variableness, neither shadow of turning. **18** Of his own will begat he us with the word of truth, that we should be a kind of firstfruits of his creatures. **19** Wherefore, my beloved brethren, let every man be swift to hear, slow to speak, slow to wrath: **20** For the wrath of man worketh not the righteousness of God. KJV

Anger is first of all harmful to you, and then to all around you, It will destroy relationships and cause you great sorrow for the words you have spoken. Determine in your heart not to let the sun go down on your wrath. My wife and I made that decision many years ago, and we believe it played a big part in our marriage lasting all those years (62 years before she went home to be with the Lord). We decided to not go to sleep angry at each other, oh there were a few long nights mostly in the first two years, but not many, and none since then.

BE KIND TO EACH OTHER, AND IN EVERY RELATIONSHIP, AND HAVE A GREAT DAY.

"IN GOD WE TRUST"

May 3

HAVE NO FEAR

2 Tim 1:7-10

7 For God hath not given us the spirit of fear; but of power, and of love, and of a sound mind. **8** Be not thou therefore ashamed of the testimony of our Lord, nor of me his prisoner: but be thou partaker of the afflictions of the gospel according to the power of God; **9** Who hath saved us, and called us with an holy calling, not according to our works, but according to his own purpose and grace, which was given us in Christ Jesus before the world began, **10** But is now made manifest by the appearing of our Saviour Jesus Christ, who hath abolished death, and hath brought life and immortality to light through the gospel: KJV

Have no fear, fear is not a gift from God, but from the enemy, (Satan.} Take your gift of faith and power, resist or reject fear and it will not control you. When fear knocks at your door, let your faith answer and there will be no one there. Your gift from God is power, love and a sound mind. So submit yourself to God, and resist the devil, and he will flee from you.

DON'T LET FEAR CONTROL YOU, HAVE A GREAT DAY.

"IN GOD WE TRUST"

MAY 4

A MERRY HEART IS LIKE A MEDICINE

Prov 15:11-13

11 Hell and destruction are before the Lord: how much more then the hearts of the children of men? **12** A scorner loveth not one that reproveth him: neither will he go unto the wise. **13** A merry heart maketh a cheerful countenance: but by sorrow of the heart the spirit is broken. KJV

A merry heart acts like a medicine for you. Don't let worry, sorrow, and sadness overtake you, determine that you are going to be glad and rejoice, even when you don't feel like it, for the joy of the Lord is your strength, it brings a smile to your face, and joy in your heart, and prosperity in every area of your life.

LAUGH AND THE WORLD LAUGHS WITH YOU.

"IN GOD WE TRUST"

Pastor Ray

MAY 5

DON'T GIVE UP HOPE

Proverbs 13:12

12 Hope deferred maketh the heart sick: but when the desire cometh, it is a tree of life. The King James Version, (Cambridge: Cambridge) 1769.

Hope is the blue print of what you are believing for, and when you begin to give up hope it is like a blue print when the lines have started to fade and you are no longer able to make out the desired object. It is like when our vision is blurred, you are hoping for something that you do not have a clear picture of inside of you. KEEP YOUR HOPE UP, AND YOUR VISION SHARP UNTIL YOU HAVE RECEIVED WHAT YOU ARE HOPING FOR. DON'T GIVE UP ON GOD, HE NEVER GAVE UP ON YOU.

THEN LET YOUR JOY OVERFLOW, AND HAVE A NICE DAY.

"IN GOD WE TRUST"

MAY 6

LOVE ONE ANOTHER

Prov 3:1-2

My son, forget not my law; but let thine heart keep my commandments: **2** For length of days, and long life, and peace, shall they add to thee. KJV

Prov 3:1-2

MY SON, forget not my law *or* teaching, but let your heart keep my commandments; **2** For length of days and years of a life [worth living] and tranquility [inward and outward and continuing through old age till death], these shall they add to you. AMP

God's commandments are His love for us, each one is filled with His love and a promise, that if we will be obedient, we will receive the promise, I Praise God for His promise of a long life worth living, for I am receiving that promise even today, as I celebrate my 87th year of life, thanking Him that I can play golf, live alone, drive my car, get around good, and spread His and my love to all of my Children, Grand Children, Great grand Children, and friends. full filling His command to love one another, John 15:12 KJV 12 This is my commandment, That ye love one another, as I have loved you.

RECEIVE HIS AND MY LOVE, AND HAVE A GREAT DAY.

"IN GOD WE TRUST"

Pastor Ray

MAY 7

YOU ARE AVERY SPECIAL

John 15:15-16

15 Henceforth I call you not servants; for the servant knoweth not what his lord doeth: but I have called you friends; for all things that I have heard of my Father I have made known unto you. **16** Ye have not chosen me, but I have chosen you, and ordained you, that ye should go and bring forth fruit, and that your fruit should remain: that whatsoever ye shall ask of the Father in my name, he may give it you. KJV

You are very special to God for He knew that your heart would let His love flow through you to those around you. He picked you out of the crowd to be His, so that He could love you, and have the fruit of His Spirit (love) produced in abundance in your life, then whatever you ask for in the name of Jesus, He can trust you enough to give it to you. Why? because you are producing the fruit of His Spirit that remains. Galatians 5:22-23 22 But the fruit of the Spirit is love, joy, peace, longsuffering, gentleness, goodness, faith, 23 Meekness, temperance: against such there is no law. KJV

LET GOD'S LOVE FLOW THROUGH YOU, AND HAVE A GREAT DAY

"IN GOD WE TRUST"

MAY 8

LOVE ONE ANOTHER

Prov 3:1-2

My son, forget not my law; but let thine heart keep my commandments: **2** For length of days, and long life, and peace, shall they add to thee. KJV

Prov 3:1-2

MY SON, forget not my law *or* teaching, but let your heart keep my commandments; **2** For length of days and years of a life [worth living] and tranquility [inward and outward and continuing through old age till death], these shall they add to you. AMP

God's commandments are His love for us, each one is filled with His love and a promise, that if we will be obedient, we will receive the promise, I Praise God for His promise of a long life worth living, for I am receiving that promise even today, as I celebrate my 87th year of life, thanking Him that I can play golf, live alone, drive my car, get around good, and spread His and my love to all of my Children, Grand Children, Great grand Children, and friends. full filling His command to love one another, John 15:12 KJV 12 This is my commandment, That ye love one another, as I have loved you.

RECEIVE HIS AND MY LOVE, AND HAVE A GREAT DAY.

"IN GOD WE TRUST"

MAY 9

A MARK YOU DO NOT WANT

Rev 13:16-18

16 And he causeth all, both small and great, rich and poor, free and bond, to receive a mark in their right hand, or in their foreheads: **17** And that no man might buy or sell, save he that had the mark, or the name of the beast, or the number of his name. **18** Here is wisdom. Let him that hath understanding count the number of the beast: for it is the number of a man; and his number is Six hundred threescore and six. KJV

A mark or tattoo you really do not want on your body, be cautious about permanent marks being put on your body, don't let Satan use you as a walking bill board for his messages, some times pictures speak louder than words,

STAY CLEAN, HAVE A NICE DAY

"IN GOD WE TRUST"

MAY 10

DO YOU WANT SAFETY?

Prov 18:8-10

8 The words of a talebearer are as wounds, and they go down into the innermost parts of the belly. **9** He also that is slothful in his work is brother to him that is a great waster. **10** The name of the Lord is a strong tower: the righteous runneth into it, and is safe.

KJV

God always has his arm outstretched for you to run into, He loves to be able to put His arms around you and comfort you when you need help, no matter what the problem may be. You should always run to Him, not from Him, as He is always there waiting for you to make the move towards Him so that He can respond with the magnitude of His love. Notice that the scripture says that the good CAN run to God's safe place. His purpose is to never leave you nor forsake you, and get you to the position that you never leave nor forsake Him.

RUN TO YOUR SAFE PLACE, AND HAVE A GREAT DAY.

"IN GOD WE TRUST"

MAY 11

GOD WANTS YOU
TO HAVE A GOOD LIFE

Proverbs 21:21

21 He that followeth after righteousness and mercy findeth life, righteousness, and honour.

The King James Version, (Cambridge: Cambridge) 1769.

Prov 21:21

Whoever goes hunting for what is right and kind finds life itself—glorious life!

(from THE MESSAGE: The Bible in Contemporary Language © 2002 by Eugene H. Peterson. All rights reserved.)

We are told in Proverbs 3:1-2 that if we keep His commandments we will have a long life worth living, that means with peace, Love, righteousness, and honor, finding favor with God and man.

SEEK AND YOU WILL FIND, LISTEN AND YOU WILL HEAR. HAVE A NICE DAY.

"IN GOD WE TRUST"

Pastor Ray

MAY 12

GODS COVENANT PROMISES ARE FOR YOU

Deut 8:17-18

17 And thou say in thine heart, My power and the might of mine hand hath gotten me this wealth. **18** But thou shalt remember the Lord thy God: for it is he that giveth thee power to get wealth, that he may establish his covenant which he sware unto thy fathers, as it is this day.

KJV

With a promise like this how can we begin to think that God does not want us to be prosperous in every area of our life. Even though the covenant was made with our ancestors, it is for us this day, so receive the power to get wealth and put it work in your life. It is your heritage, but remember who gave it to you. The purpose of this gift is to establish His covenant with you.

BELIEVE, RECEIVE, AND PUT IT TO WORK. HAVE A HAPPY AND PROSPEROUS DAY.

"IN GOD WE TRUST"

MAY 13

GODS GIFT TO YOU, HEALTH

1 Peter 2:21-24

21 For even hereunto were ye called: because Christ also suffered for us, leaving us an example, that ye should follow his steps: **22** Who did no sin, neither was guile found in his mouth: **23** Who, when he was reviled, reviled not again; when he suffered, he threatened not; but committed himself to him that judgeth righteously: **24** Who his own self bare our sins in his own body on the tree, that we, being dead to sins, should live unto righteousness: by whose stripes ye were healed. KJV

Health is yours as a free gift from God, bought and paid for, debt free. Notice the word "were", it is past tense which means that you already have been healed and health is yours. Don't let anyone steal from you what is yours, it is paid for and given to you. Fight to keep it. It is like having money in the bank and refusing to write a check when you are hungry and don't have the cash on hand to buy food. Submit yourself to God, resist the devil and he will flee from you.

DON'T LET SATAN STEAL FROM YOU, HAVE A GREAT DAY

"IN GOD WE TRUST"

MAY 14

BE NOT AFRAID

Deut 20:1-4

When thou goest out to battle against thine enemies, and seest horses, and chariots, and a people more than thou, be not afraid of them: for the Lord thy God is with thee, which brought thee up out of the land of Egypt. **2** And it shall be, when ye are come nigh unto the battle, that the priest shall approach and speak unto the people, **3** And shall say unto them, Hear, O Israel, ye approach this day unto battle against your enemies: let not your hearts faint, fear not, and do not tremble, neither be ye terrified because of them; **4** For the Lord your God is he that goeth with you, to fight for you against your enemies, to save you. KJV

As you begin this new week do not be afraid to put your trust and faith in God, for He is with you through every trial, battle and circumstance. He is with you every step of the way to victory, He is fighting with you to win.

TRUST GOD, HE WILL MAKE YOU A WINNER. HAVE A GREAT DAY

IN GOD WE TRUST"

Pastor Ray

MAY 15

HOW TO GET YOUR PRAYERS ANSWERED

John 15:5-8

5 I am the vine, ye are the branches: He that abideth in me, and I in him, the same bringeth forth much fruit: for without me ye can do nothing. **6** If a man abide not in me, he is cast forth as a branch, and is withered; and men gather them, and cast them into the fire, and they are burned. **7** If ye abide in me, and my words abide in you, ye shall ask what ye will, and it shall be done unto you. **8** Herein is my Father glorified, that ye bear much fruit; so shall ye be my disciples. KJV

When we put God and His Word first place in our lives, and truly believe what He says in His word, then we will receive because we believe. Fill yourself with His Word, stay hooked up to Him, this is the way we abide in Him, and by being full of His Word He abides in us. And our prayers will be answered.

PRAY, BELIEVE, AND RECEIVE. HAVE A GREAT DAY.

"IN GOD WE TRUST"

Pastor Ray

MAY 16

YOU HAVE HELP WITH YOUR CARES

1 Peter 5:7-10

7 Casting all your care upon him; for he careth for you. **8** Be sober, be vigilant; because your adversary the devil, as a roaring lion, walketh about, seeking whom he may devour: **9** Whom resist stedfast in the faith, knowing that the same afflictions are accomplished in your brethren that are in the world. **10** But the God of all grace, who hath called us unto his eternal glory by Christ Jesus, after that ye have suffered a while, make you perfect, stablish, strengthen, settle you. KJV

Let God help you through your trials and troubles, go to Him in prayer making your need known to Him, then leave them there with Him, for He loves you and cares for you.

GOD HAS THE LAST WORD, KNOW THE HE LOVES YOU. HAVE A GREAT DAY

"IN GOD WE TRUST"

MAY 17

GOD IS ON YOUR SIDE

Rom 8:29-31

29 For whom he did foreknow, he also did predestinate to be conformed to the image of his Son, that he might be the firstborn among many brethren. **30** Moreover whom he did predestinate, them he also called: and whom he called, them he also justified: and whom he justified, them he also glorified. **31** What shall we then say to these things? If God be for us, who can be against us? KJV

When God is for us we have an army of His angels around us to see that we are protected. Our part is to rest assured that God means what He says, have faith in Him, and know that He is able to stand behind His Word to perform it.

TRUST HIM, AND HAVE A LOVELY DAY.

"IN GOD WE TRUST"

MAY 18

GOD WANTS YOU TO HAVE A SAFE LIFE

Prov 20:1,24,29

Wine is a mocker, strong drink is raging: and whosoever is deceived thereby is not wise. 24 Man's goings are of the Lord; how can a man then understand his own way? 29 The glory of young men is their strength: and the beauty of old men is the gray head. KJV

When we go our own way, doing the things we think we enjoy, we will usually wind up not feeling good about it, but if we let God direct our steps He will keep us going in the right direction to reach an expected end and spend eternity with Him.

LET GOD LEAD, AND HAVE A GREAT DAY.

"IN GOD WE TRUST"

Pastor Ray

MAY 19

LET GO AND LET GOD

Matt 5:43-47

43 Ye have heard that it hath been said, Thou shalt love thy neighbour, and hate thine enemy. **44** But I say unto you, Love your enemies, bless them that curse you, do good to them that hate you, and pray for them which despitefully use you, and persecute you; **45** That ye may be the children of your Father which is in heaven: for he maketh his sun to rise on the evil and on the good, and sendeth rain on the just and on the unjust. **46** For if ye love them which love you, what reward have ye? do not even the publicans the same? **47** And if ye salute your brethren only, what do ye more than others? do not even the publicans so?

If you will let go and pray for those who mistreat you and let God handle it, as He can do a much better job than you or I can, then His peace which passes all understanding will flood over you, as you realize that God loves you and is more than able to take care of your problems.

LET GO AND LET GOD. BELIEVE AND RECEIVE. HAVE A NICE DAY

"IN GOD WE TRUST"

MAY 20

YOU ARE FORGIVEN

Ephesians 4:29-32

29 Let no corrupt communication proceed out of your mouth, but that which is good to the use of edifying, that it may minister grace unto the hearers. 30 And grieve not the holy Spirit of God, whereby ye are sealed unto the day of redemption. 31 Let all bitterness, and wrath, and anger, and clamour, and evil speaking, be put away from you, with all malice: 32 And be ye kind one to another, tenderhearted, forgiving one another, even as God for Christ's sake hath forgiven you.

The King James Version, (Cambridge: Cambridge) 1769.

Un-forgiveness will cause anger to be present in your heart, and out of the abundance of the heart your mouth speaks. Again let go and let God, forgive for you are forgiven. Notice the word hath, which is past tense, which means it is already done.

YOU ARE FORGIVEN. HAVE A GREAT DAY.

"IN GOD WE TRUST"

Pastor Ray

MAY 21

MAKE YOUR PARENTS HAPPY

Prov 23:22-25

22 Hearken unto thy father that begat thee, and despise not thy mother when she is old. **23** Buy the truth, and sell it not; also wisdom, and instruction, and understanding. **24** The father of the righteous shall greatly rejoice: and he that begetteth a wise child shall have joy of him. **25** Thy father and thy mother shall be glad, and she that bare thee shall rejoice. KJV

Mothers day has just passed, and Fathers day will soon be here. your children will see how you show love and respect for your parents, and will treat you the way your actions taught them. what your children see in you, they will reproduce. Actions speak louder than words.

LOVE GOES A LONG WAY. HAVE A GREAT DAY.

"IN GOD WE TRUST"

Pastor Ray

MAY 22

GOOD THINGS ARE COMING YOUR WAY

Jer 29:11-13

11 For I know the thoughts that I think toward you, saith the Lord, thoughts of peace, and not of evil, to give you an expected end. **12** Then shall ye call upon me, and ye shall go and pray unto me, and I will hearken unto you. **13** And ye shall seek me, and find me, when ye shall search for me with all your heart. KJV

God shows His love toward us in many ways. The more we yield to Him the easier it is for Him to fulfill the plans He has for us, plans for good things, not bad.

SOMETHING GOOD IS COMING YOUR WAY. HAVE A NICE DAY

"IN GOD WE TRUST"

Pastor Ray

MAY 23

YOU ARE A VERY SPECIAL PERSON

Zeph 3:16-17

16 In that day it shall be said to Jerusalem, Fear thou not: and to Zion, Let not thine hands be slack. **17** The Lord thy God in the midst of thee is mighty; he will save, he will rejoice over thee with joy; he will rest in his love, he will joy over thee with singing. KJV

God has always loved you, even when you thought He did not know you existed. His heart is saddened when we get out from under His umbrella of protection, but he rejoices when we come back home to Him. Put your name in the place of Jerusalem, And let His love flood over you, wiping away all of your fears and anxieties.

RELAX, AND ENJOY YOUR DAY.

"IN GOD WE TRUST"

Pastor Ray

MAY 24

HOLD YOUR HEAD HIGH

Luke 21:25-28

25 And there shall be signs in the sun, and in the moon, and in the stars; and upon the earth distress of nations, with perplexity; the sea and the waves roaring; **26** Men's hearts failing them for fear, and for looking after those things which are coming on the earth: for the powers of heaven shall be shaken. **27** And then shall they see the Son of man coming in a cloud with power and great glory. **28** And when these things begin to come to pass, then look up, and lift up your heads; for your redemption draweth nigh. KJV

We may ask what things? The day of the vengeance of the Lord. When we see these times we know that we should look up and hold our heads up for our redemption draweth neigh. We don't have to wait until the end times for God will give us our redemption when we ask. Hold your head up, be not ashamed, you are redeemed when you ask.

ASK, AND YOUR HELP IS ON THE WAY, HAVE A GREAT DAY.

"IN GOD WE TRUST"

Pastor Ray

MAY 25

BE DILIGENT

Prov 27:23-27

23 Be thou diligent to know the state of thy flocks, and look well to thy herds. **24** For riches are not for ever: and doth the crown endure to every generation? **25** The hay appeareth, and the tender grass sheweth itself, and herbs of the mountains are gathered. **26** The lambs are for thy clothing, and the goats are the price of the field. **27** And thou shalt have goats' milk enough for thy food, for the food of thy household, and for the maintenance for thy maidens. KJV

Gods desire for you is to have more than enough, so guard your friends, investments, and possessions, be generous with your affections, share, or give and it shall be given to you good measure pressed down and shaken together shall your family, and friends give love and fellowship to you, for what ever a person sows that shall they also harvest.

WALK IN LOVE, AND HAVE A GREAT DAY.

"IN GOD WE TRUST"

MAY 26

BE A SEEKER

Prov 28:5-6

5 Evil men understand not judgment: but they that seek the Lord understand all things. **6** Better is the poor that walketh in his uprightness, than he that is perverse in his ways, though he be rich. KJV

God knows who we are and how to get in touch with us, and He knows where and what He wants us to do and be, God says in Jer 29:11, I know what I'm doing. I have it all planned out—plans to take care of you, not abandon you, plans to give you the future you hope for. (The Message Bible)

BE A SEEKER, FIND GOD AND LIVE WELL, HAVE A GREAT WEEK END.

"IN GOD WE TRUST"

Pastor Ray

MAY 27

GODS WAY IS JOY

Job 8:19-22

19 Behold, this is the joy of his way, and out of the earth shall others grow. 20 Behold, God will not cast away a perfect man, neither will he help the evil doers: 21 Till he fill thy mouth with laughing, and thy lips with rejoicing. 22 They that hate thee shall be clothed with shame; and the dwelling place of the wicked shall come to nought.

The King James Version, (Cambridge: Cambridge) 1769.

God cares for those who love him, He will let his joy fill you, put your enemies to shame and bring you out on top with joy and laughter in your heart, and your lips rejoicing.

HAVE A GREAT MEMORIAL DAY

"IN GOD WE TRUST"

Pastor Ray

MAY 28

LET GOD LIFT YOU UP

Prov 30:5-6, 32-33

5 Every word of God is pure: he is a shield unto them that put their trust in him. **6** Add thou not unto his words, lest he reprove thee, and thou be found a liar. :**32** If thou hast done foolishly in lifting up thyself, or if thou hast thought evil, lay thine hand upon thy mouth. **33** Surely the churning of milk bringeth forth butter, and the wringing of the nose bringeth forth blood: so the forcing of wrath bringeth forth strife. KJV

Let God or others lift you up, or praise you, as we celebrate this Memorial holiday let us praise our present military personnel for their courage and sacrifice, and remember those of other wars that our country has been involved in that have laid down their lives for our freedom. and remember

FREEDOM IS NOT CHEAP. HAVE A GREAT HOLIDAY

"IN GOD WE TRUST"

Pastor Ray

MAY 29

YOUR JOY CAN BE FULL

Ps 16:9-11

9 Therefore my heart is glad, and my glory rejoiceth: my flesh also shall rest in hope. **10** For thou wilt not leave my soul in hell; neither wilt thou suffer thine Holy One to see corruption. **11** Thou wilt shew me the path of life: in thy presence is fulness of joy; at thy right hand there are pleasures for evermore. KJV

This is the position God wants us to be in, close to Him, in His presence, so that our hearts can be glad, and that we can have fullness of joy and pleasure for evermore. He is our Father God and wishes to share our joy and pleasure, because when our joy is full it gives Him great pleasure.

REST IN HOPE, AND HAVE A GREAT MEMORIAL DAY. REMEMBER, GODS LOVE FOR YOU IS UNCONDITIONAL.

"IN GOD WE TRUST"

Pastor Ray

MAY 30

LET GOD BE YOUR SHIELD

Prov 30:5-6

5 Every word of God is pure: he is a shield unto them that put their trust in Him.

6 Add thou not unto his words, lest he reprove thee, and thou be found a liar. KJV

Prov 30:5-6

5 Every word of God is tried *and* purified; He is a shield to those who trust *and* take refuge in Him. [Ps 18:30; 84:11; 115:9-11.] **6** Add not to His words, lest He reprove you, and you be found a liar. AMP

Put your trust in God and His Word and let no untrue words pass through you lips so that you can be sure that He is your shield and protector.

WHEN WE TRUST IN GOD, WE CAN HAVE A GREAT DAY.

"IN GOD WE TRUST"

MAY 31

MEN, LOVE YOUR WIFE

Prov 31:10-12

10 Who can find a virtuous woman? for her price is far above rubies. **11** The heart of her husband doth safely trust in her, so that he shall have no need of spoil. **12** She will do him good and not evil all the days of her life.

KJV

Prov 31:10-12

10 A capable, intelligent, *and* virtuous woman—who is he who can find her? She is far more precious than jewels *and* her value is far above rubies *or* pearls. [Prov 12:4; 18:22; 19:14.] **11** The heart of her husband trusts in her confidently *and* relies on and believes in her securely, so that he has no lack of [honest] gain or need of [dishonest] spoil. **12** She comforts, encourages, *and* does him only good as long as there is life within her. AMP

Your wife is not only your helper she is your rib come home to make you complete, to have your arm around her, having her close to your heart to be protected and loved so she can fulfill her calling from God to be your virtuous woman.

DON'T GIVE HER UP, HAVE A GREAT DAY.

"IN GOD WE TRUST"

Pastor Ray

JUNE 1

BELIEVE AND RECEIVE

John 14:12-14

12 Verily, verily, I say unto you, He that believeth on me, the works that I do shall he do also; and greater works than these shall he do; because I go unto my Father. **13** And whatsoever ye shall ask in my name, that will I do, that the Father may be glorified in the Son. **14** If ye shall ask any thing in my name, I will do it.

KJV

God wants you blessed, happy, and prosperous, read these scriptures again and let them soak into your heart knowing that God can do what He promises, His promise here is get right with God, then pray in the name of Jesus.

STAY IN RIGHT STANDING WITH GOD, PRAY, TRUST AND RECEIVE.

"IN GOD WE TRUST"

Pastor Ray

JUNE 2

GOD HAS A PLACE FOR YOU

John 14:1-4

Let not your heart be troubled: ye believe in God, believe also in me. **2** In my Father's house are many mansions: if it were not so, I would have told you. I go to prepare a place for you. **3** And if I go and prepare a place for you, I will come again, and receive you unto myself; that where I am, there ye may be also. **4** And whither I go ye know, and the way ye know. KJV

Jesus has a place prepared for you in God's house, and it is a mansion fully furnished with the best, all you have to do is believe and receive it. Your destination is established, walk with God and get there safely.

LET GOD LEAD, AND HAVE A GREAT DAY.

"IN GOD WE TRUST"

Pastor Ray

June 3

LET THE POWER OF GOD SEE YOU THROUGH

Eph 6:10-12

10 Finally, my brethren, be strong in the Lord, and in the power of his might. **11** Put on the whole armour of God, that ye may be able to stand against the wiles of the devil. **12** For we wrestle not against flesh and blood, but against principalities, against powers, against the rulers of the darkness of this world, against spiritual wickedness in high places. KJV

When our all mighty God is standing behind us, there is no power on earth that can stand against Him. And when we are dressed in God's armor, the Devil will run from us. Why? Because when we are fully dressed in God's armor and close the face plate on our helmet of salvation, he has no way of knowing who is in there and he has been whipped once by the guy wearing that armor and does not want to be whipped again. HE IS A DEFEATED FOE, BUT WILL TRY TO DECEIVE US INTO THINKING HE IS NOT.

DON'T BE DECEIVED, HAVE A PROSPEROUS DAY

"IN GOD WE TRUST"

Pastor Ray

JUNE 4

THERE IS WARFARE GOING ON

Eph 6:13-18

13 Wherefore take unto you the whole armour of God, that ye may be able to withstand in the evil day, and having done all, to stand. **14** Stand therefore, having your loins girt about with truth, and having on the breastplate of righteousness; **15** And your feet shod with the preparation of the gospel of peace; **16** Above all, taking the shield of faith, wherewith ye shall be able to quench all the fiery darts of the wicked. **17** And take the helmet of salvation, and the sword of the Spirit, which is the word of God: **18** Praying always with all prayer and supplication in the Spirit, and watching thereunto with all perseverance and supplication for all saints; KJV

Don't forget even one piece of God's armor. You would not go to work wearing only one shoe, or a half of a coat, a tie with no shirt. So don't leave home without the full armor of God, when you are fully clothed in God's armor, the enemy cannot touch you. Remember all the devil has are fiery darts, which are thoughts, Isn't it great to know that you have the victory in Jesus.

TAKE NO THOUGHT SAYING. HAVE A VICTORIOUS DAY.

"IN GOD WE TRUST"

Pastor Ray

JUNE 5

GOD IS ON YOUR SIDE

Deut 4:29-31

29 But if from thence thou shalt seek the Lord thy God, thou shalt find him, if thou seek him with all thy heart and with all thy soul. **30** When thou art in tribulation, and all these things are come upon thee, even in the latter days, if thou turn to the Lord thy God, and shalt be obedient unto his voice; **31** (For the Lord thy God is a merciful God;) he will not forsake thee, neither destroy thee, nor forget the covenant of thy fathers which he sware unto them. KJV

It is never to late, A friend of mine lay dieing on his bathroom floor, and gave his heart to God, and spent the last 15 minutes of his life telling his wife how beautiful heaven is. When hard times come, run to God, don't run from Him. He promised long ago that He would be merciful if we would return to Him and that He would not forsake us. Know that He is with you always, even when you don't feel like He is. He waits with open arms for you to come to Him.

DON'T WAIT UNTIL THE END. HAVE A GREAT DAY

"IN GOD WE TRUST"

Pastor Ray

JUNE 6

GOD HEARS YOUR PRAYERS

Ps 6:8-10

8 Depart from me, all ye workers of iniquity; for the Lord hath heard the voice of my weeping. **9** The Lord hath heard my supplication; the Lord will receive my prayer. **10** Let all mine enemies be ashamed and sore vexed: let them return and be ashamed suddenly. KJV

God is on your side, He listens when you talk, and when you get in right standing with Him, He will hear your prayer request and answer them. God will not leave you helpless, don't listen to the Devil's lies, he can do nothing to you without you permission, the Devil is limited to what you allow him to do.

GOD HAS YOUR BACK, HAVE A GREAT DAY.

"IN GOD WE TRUST"

Pastor Ray

JUNE 7

LET YOUR HEART BE MERRY

Proverbs 17:22

22 A merry heart doeth good like a medicine: but a broken spirit drieth the bones. KJV

Laugh and the world laughs with you, so they say. God says a merry heart is like a medicine to you, it makes you feel good, and fills you with joy and causes those around you to rejoice with you.

HAVE A HAPPY DAY.

"IN GOD WE TRUST"

JUNE 8

MONEY IS NOT EVERYTHING

Prov 8:8-11

8 All the words of my mouth are in righteousness; there is nothing froward or perverse in them. **9** They are all plain to him that understandeth, and right to them that find knowledge. **10** Receive my instruction, and not silver; and knowledge rather than choice gold. **11** For wisdom is better than rubies; and all the things that may be desired are not to be compared to it. KJV

Prov 8:8-11

8 All the words of my mouth are righteous (upright and in right standing with God); there is nothing contrary to truth or crooked in them. **9** They are all plain to him who understands [and opens his heart], and right to those who find knowledge [and live by it]. **10** Receive my instruction in preference to [striving for] silver, and knowledge rather than choice gold, **11** For skillful *and* godly Wisdom is better than rubies *or* pearls, and all the things that may be desired are not to be compared to it. [Job 28:15; Ps 19:10; 119:127.] AMP

Finding God's knowledge and receiving His instructions will put you in the right place at the right time, to receive His blessings, one which is to give you the desires of you heart. Wealth is a by product of doing what you love to do.

BELIEVE AND RECEIVE, HAVE A GREAT DAY

"IN GOD WE TRUST"

Pastor Ray

JUNE 9

YOUR ARE BEAUTIFUL IN GODS EYES

2 Cor 5:16-19

16 Wherefore henceforth know we no man after the flesh: yea, though we have known Christ after the flesh, yet now henceforth know we him no more. **17** Therefore if any man be in Christ, he is a new creature: old things are passed away; behold, all things are become new. **18** And all things are of God, who hath reconciled us to himself by Jesus Christ, and hath given to us the ministry of reconciliation; **19** To wit, that God was in Christ, reconciling the world unto himself, not imputing their trespasses unto them; and hath committed unto us the word of reconciliation. KJV

Did you ever hear the song, This old House? Or see someone buy an old house to fix up. That person doesn't see the house as it is, but as it will be when he is finished with it. God is the same with us, He takes us just the way we are, then proceeds to change us into the finished product that only He can see, a beautiful creature created in His Image.

GOD SEES YOU AS A BEAUTIFUL NEW CREATION. HAVE A GREAT DAY.

"IN GOD WE TRUST"

Pastor Ray

JUNE 10

DOES IT SEEM LIKE THERE IS NEVER ENOUGH?

Prov 3:9-12

9 Honour the Lord with thy substance, and with the firstfruits of all thine increase: **10** So shall thy barns be filled with plenty, and thy presses shall burst out with new wine. **11** My son, despise not the chastening of the Lord; neither be weary of his correction: **12** For whom the Lord loveth he correcteth; even as a father the son in whom he delighteth. KJV

God promises that if we will honor Him. Put Him first place in our lives, that He will put us first place with Him, and see to it that we are well supplied in every area to over flowing, having more than enough to share with others. God wants His love and wealth to flow through us to others and when it does there will be plenty of everything left for us. health, and wealth is for you today.

GOD HAS NOT FORGOT HIS PROMISE. HAVE A GREAT DAY

"IN GOD WE TRUST"

Pastor Ray

JUNE 11

FEAR NOT

Deut 31:6

6 Be strong and of a good courage, fear not, nor be afraid of them: for the Lord thy God, he it is that doth go with thee; he will not fail thee, nor forsake thee.

KJV

Don't let the enemy intimidate you, stay on the course that God has impressed you to take, don't turn to the left or right but go straight ahead to the goal before you, knowing that God is with you all the time, and He will bring you through to victory.

STAY THE COURSE. HAVE A GREAT DAY.

In His Love

"IN GOD WE TRUST"

Pastor Ray

JUNE 12

GOD'S LOVE TO YOU, AND THROUGH YOU

John 3:16-18

16 For God so loved the world, that he gave his only begotten Son, that whosoever believeth in him should not perish, but have everlasting life. **17** For God sent not his Son into the world to condemn the world; but that the world through him might be saved. **18** He that believeth on him is not condemned: but he that believeth not is condemned already, because he hath not believed in the name of the only begotten Son of God. KJV

As you go through the day you are afforded many opportunities to show the love of God flowing through you. As you see a person in need you can stop and help or ignore the situation. The need you see could be many things, loneliness, money, physical help, etc. When you see or know a need, don't ignore God's call to your heart to help.

YOUR REWARD WILL BE GREAT. HAVE A NICE DAY.

"IN GOD WE TRUST"

Pastor Ray

JUNE 13

BE FILLED WITH GOD'S LOVE

Prov 13:10-12

10 Only by pride cometh contention: but with the well advised is wisdom. **11** Wealth gotten by vanity shall be diminished: but he that gathereth by labour shall increase.**12** Hope deferred maketh the heart sick: but when the desire cometh, it is a tree of life. KJV

Let the love of God fill your heart with righteous desires, that He may full fill those desires of your heart, and bring joy to your heart, a smile to your face, and prosperity in every area of you life.

GOOD BREAKS ARE COMING YOUR WAY. HAVE A GREAT DAY, AND A GREAT WEEK.

"IN GOD WE TRUST"

Pastor Ray

JUNE 14

LET THE PEACE OF GOD KEEP YOUR HEART

Phil 4:4-7

4 Rejoice in the Lord alway: and again I say, Rejoice. 5 Let your moderation be known unto all men. The Lord is at hand. 6 Be careful for nothing; but in every thing by prayer and supplication with thanksgiving let your requests be made known unto God. 7 And the peace of God, which passeth all understanding, shall keep your hearts and minds through Christ Jesus. KJV

God has already made provisions for us to have His peace. Our part is to go to Him in prayer with thanksgiving in our hearts, and faith in Him that He is able and willing to grant our request. He loves you as a father, for He has chosen you to be in His family. Children translated into the kingdom of His dear Son, and wants you to let His peace keep your heart and mind.

PRAY AND RECEIVE. HAVE A GREAT DAY

"IN GOD WE TRUST"

Pastor Ray

JUNE 15

GODS MERCY TO YOU IS EVERLASTING

Psalm 100:3-5

3 Know ye that the LORD he is God: it is he that hath made us, and not we ourselves; we are his people, and the sheep of his pasture. 4 Enter into his gates with thanksgiving, and into his courts with praise: be thankful unto him, and bless his name. 5 For the LORD is good; his mercy is everlasting; and his truth endureth to all generations.

The King James Version, (Cambridge: Cambridge) 1769.

I am very thankful today that God's mercy endures forever. He waited fifty years for me to wake up and know who He is. And now I am thankful for the peace that He gives me in all situations. He is no respecter of persons His forgiveness is extended to us all regardless of how bad we have been. His desire is that none should perish. Open your heart today and let Him give you the piece that is beyond our understanding.

BE STILL AND KNOW THAT HE IS GOD. HAVE A GOOD DAY

"IN GOD WE TRUST"

Pastor Ray

JUNE 16

GOD IS HERE FOR YOU

Ps 16:2-4

2 O my soul, thou hast said unto the Lord, Thou art my Lord: my goodness extendeth not to thee; **3** But to the saints that are in the earth, and to the excellent, in whom is all my delight. **4** Their sorrows shall be multiplied that hasten after another god: their drink offerings of blood will I not offer, nor take up their names into my lips. KJV

God has heard your cries and has come to be with you, to hold your hand and see you through to victory over all of your trials and tribulations, to place you above and not beneath, to set you on the high places, not leave you in the valley.

LET GOD IN AND TRUST HIM. HAVE A GREAT DAY

"IN GOD WE TRUST"

Pastor Ray

JUNE 17

FOLLOW GOD

Ps 17:4-5

4 Concerning the works of men, by the word of thy lips I have kept me from the paths of the destroyer. **5** Hold up my goings in thy paths, that my footsteps slip not. KJV

Do it God's way and be sure that where He leads, you will follow, keeping your feet on the solid path where you will not slip and fall, let Him lead you to your destination.

DON'T GIVE UP, TRUST GOD AND WIN. HAVE A GREAT DAY

"IN GOD WE TRUST"

JUNE 18

YOU ARE A CHOSEN ONE

John 15:16-17

16 Ye have not chosen me, but I have chosen you, and ordained you, that ye should go and bring forth fruit, and that your fruit should remain: that whatsoever ye shall ask of the Father in my name, he may give it you. **17** These things I command you, that ye love one another. KJV

Jesus has chosen you because He loves you to much to leave you the way you are. He will constantly mold and shape you into the person He wants you to be, and when you get there He has given you the power to use His name to ask and receive of the Father God. Let His plan for you be completed.

BELIEVE AND RECEIVE. HAVE A GREAT WEEK.

"IN GOD WE TRUST"

Pastor Ray

JUNE 19

YOU ARE MORE THAN CONQUERORS

Romans 8:35-37

35 Who shall separate us from the love of Christ? shall tribulation, or distress, or persecution, or famine, or nakedness, or peril, or sword? 36 As it is written, For thy sake we are killed all the day long; we are accounted as sheep for the slaughter. 37 Nay, in all these things we are more than conquerors through him that loved us.

The King James Version, (Cambridge: Cambridge) 1769.

In Jesus we have the victory. We should do everything in our power to stay hooked up with Him, being aware that the trials and tribulations that we get into can separate us from His love, but only if we allow it to happen. How do we let it happen? By getting into a pity party with ourselves, railing against God and blaming Him instead of ourselves, WE got into it and He will get us out if we let Him.

LET GOD HANDLE IT, HAVE A GREAT DAY.

"IN GOD WE TRUST"

June 20

GOD'S WORD IS THE SAME TODAY AND FOREVER, IF YOU WILL ONLY BELIEVE

Luke 1:26-38

26 In the sixth month of Elizabeth's pregnancy, God sent the angel Gabriel to Nazareth, a village in Galilee, 27 to a virgin named Mary. She was engaged to be married to a man named Joseph, a descendant of King David. 28 Gabriel appeared to her and said, Greetings, favored woman! The Lord is with you! 29 Confused and disturbed, Mary tried to think what the angel could mean. 30 Don't be frightened, Mary, the angel told her, for God has decided to bless you! 31 You will become pregnant and have a son, and you are to name him Jesus. 32 He will be very great and will be called the Son of the Most High. And the Lord God will give him the throne of his ancestor David. 33 And he will reign over Israel forever; his Kingdom will never end! 34 Mary asked the angel, But how can I have a baby? I am a virgin. 35 The angel replied, The Holy Spirit will come upon you, and the power of the Most High will overshadow you. So the baby born to you will be holy, and he will be called the Son of God. 36 What's more, your relative Elizabeth has become pregnant in her old age! People used to say she was barren, but she's already in her sixth month. 37 For nothing is impossible with God. 38 Mary responded, I am the Lords servant, and I am willing to accept whatever he wants. May everything you have said come true. And then the angel left.

Holy Bible, New Living Translation, (Wheaton, IL: Tyndale House Publishers, Inc.) 1996.

This is part of God's plan to reconcile to Himself His world and mankind which He created to be his friends, to walk with Him and have fellowship with Him throughout eternity. Mary heard the words of the angel, believed the words of the angel, conceived the words of the angle and brought forth the son of God, Jesus. His Word works today if we will only believe. Receive His word, become His friend, get a picture of what you are praying for in your mind, and become pregnant with it and birth it. Don't give up.

BELIEVING IS RECEIVING.

"IN GOD WE TRUST"

JUNE 21

DO YOU WANT FULLNESS OF JOY?

John 16:23-24

23 And in that day ye shall ask me nothing. Verily, verily, I say unto you, Whatsoever ye shall ask the Father in my name, he will give it you. **24** Hitherto have ye asked nothing in my name: ask, and ye shall receive, that your joy may be full.

KJV

Look to God and ask what you want and when we are at a loss and don't know which way to turn if we will remember to turn to God and not away from Him, He will show us the way to His presence where we will find fullness of joy and at His right hand, pleasures for evermore. Sounds like a place worth looking for, so give Him a chance to show you the way.

ASK AND RECEIVE.

"IN GOD WE TRUST"

Pastor Ray

JUNE 22

LONG LIFE AND PEACE

Proverbs 3:1-2

My son, forget not my law; but let thine heart keep my commandments: 2 For length of days, and long life, and peace, shall they add to thee.

The King James Version, (Cambridge: Cambridge) 1769.

If we do our part, God is faithful to do His part, give us length of days, a long life worth living, and peace beyond our wildest dreams.

GOD SAYS, "YOU DO AND I WILL, YOU DON'T AND I WONT. HAVE A GREAT DAY

"IN GOD WE TRUST"

JUNE 23

GOD WANTS YOU BLESSED

Prov 23:17-18

17 Let not thine heart envy sinners: but be thou in the fear of the Lord all the day long. **18** For surely there is an end; and thine expectation shall not be cut off. KJV

God's desire for you is that you reach the expected goals in your life, You may ask why? so that you can spend eternity with Him having received all the blessings He has provided for you.

STAY CLOSE TO GOD. HAVE A GREAT DAY.

"IN GOD WE TRUST"

JUNE 24

MY PRAYER FOR YOU

1 Cor 1:3-9

3 Grace and peace to you from God our Father and the Lord Jesus Christ.

4 I always thank God for you because of his grace given you in Christ Jesus. 5 For in him you have been enriched in every way—in all your speaking and in all your knowledge—6 because our testimony about Christ was confirmed in you. 7 Therefore you do not lack any spiritual gift as you eagerly wait for our Lord Jesus Christ to be revealed. 8 He will keep you strong to the end, so that you will be blameless on the day of our Lord Jesus Christ. 9 God, who has called you into fellowship with his Son Jesus Christ our Lord, is faithful. NIV

MAY GOD BLESS YOU FOR THE REST OF YOUR DAYS.

"IN GOD WE TRUST"

Pastor Ray

JUNE 25

GOD WANTS YOU ON HIS SIDE

Ps 25:20-22

20 O keep my soul, and deliver me: let me not be ashamed; for I put my trust in thee. **21** Let integrity and uprightness preserve me; for I wait on thee. **22** Redeem Israel, O God, out of all his troubles. KJV

God accepted you just the way you were and began the process of remaking you into the finished product He sees you to be, a vessel of honour suitable for Him to live in while you are on earth, and suitable for your residency in heaven. You could read verse 22 in the KJV like this, Redeem me O God, out of all my troubles.

JOIN GODS TEAM, HAVE A GREAT DAY

"IN GOD WE TRUST"

Pastor Ray

JUNE 26

WHEN ALL ELSE FAILS, PUT YOUR FAITH TO WORK

Mark 5:25-29

25 And there was a woman who had had a flow of blood for twelve years, **26** And who had endured much suffering under [the hands of] many physicians and had spent all that she had, and was no better but instead grew worse. **27** She had heard the reports concerning Jesus, and she came up behind Him in the throng and touched His garment, **28** For she kept saying, If I only touch His garments, I shall be restored to health. **29** And immediately her flow of blood was dried up at the source, and [suddenly] she felt in her body that she was healed of her [distressing] ailment. (Mark 5:33-34) **33** But the woman, knowing what had been done for her, though alarmed *and* frightened and trembling, fell down before Him and told Him the whole truth. **34** And He said to her, Daughter, your faith (your trust and confidence in Me, springing from faith in God) has restored you to health. Go in (into) peace and be continually healed *and* freed from your [distressing bodily] disease.

God will always do His part, if we will do ours, have faith in God. And begin with,

PUTTING YOUR FAITH TO WORK

"IN GOD WE TRUST"

Pastor Ray

JUNE 27

GOD HAS A PLACE FOR YOU

John 14:1-3

Let not your heart be troubled: ye believe in God, believe also in me. **2** In my Father's house are many mansions: if it were not so, I would have told you. I go to prepare a place for you. **3** And if I go and prepare a place for you, I will come again, and receive you unto myself; that where I am, there ye may be also. KJV

Gods love for you is never ending, He desires for you to be with Him always, and has a dwelling place prepared for you in His home. God will also come and get you to take you home with Him when your time has come.

TRUST AND FOLLOW GOD. HAVE A JOYFUL DAY.

"IN GOD WE TRUST"

Pastor Ray

JUNE 28

GOD HAS A PLAN FOR YOU

3 John 2-4

2 Beloved, I wish above all things that thou mayest prosper and be in health, even as thy soul prospereth. **3** For I rejoiced greatly, when the brethren came and testified of the truth that is in thee, even as thou walkest in the truth. **4** I have no greater joy than to hear that my children walk in truth. KJV

This is the wish of God for His children, those that believe in Him, have received Him, and been translated into the kingdom of His dear Son. He wants you to be in good health and be prosperous in all that you set your heart and mind to do.

HAVE A HAPPY AND PROSPEROUS DAY.

"IN GOD WE TRUST"

Pastor Ray

June 29

YOU CAN HAVE A WELL BALANCED MATURE LIFE?

James 1:2-4

2 My brethren, count it all joy when ye fall into divers temptations; **3** Knowing this, that the trying of your faith worketh patience. **4** But let patience have her perfect work, that ye may be perfect and entire, wanting nothing. KJV

God has made a way for you to have a full well balanced life. Resist temptations to retaliate when someone does you wrong, and above all resist the urge to participate in sinful things, God has given us the wisdom to know right from wrong.

LET PATIENCE WORK FOR YOU

"IN GOD WE TRUST"

JUNE 30

GOD IS ON YOUR SIDE

Rom 8:31-33

31 What shall we then say to these things? If God be for us, who can be against us? **32** He that spared not his own Son, but delivered him up for us all, how shall he not with him also freely give us all things? **33** Who shall lay any thing to the charge of God's elect? It is God that justifieth. KJV

God is on our side and we have an army of His angels around us to see that we are protected. Our part is to enter into His rest and know that God means what He says, have faith in Him, and know He stand behind His Word, and is able to perform it. We are told in (Mark 11:22-24) 22 "Have faith in God," Jesus answered. 23 "I tell you the truth, if anyone says to this mountain, 'Go, throw yourself into the sea,' and does not doubt in his heart but believes that what he says will happen, it will be done for him. NIV

BELIEVE AND RECEIVE: HAVE A GREAT DAY

"IN GOD WE TRUST"

Pastor Ray

JULY 1

LET THE PEACE OF GOD KEEP YOU FROM BEING AFRAID

John 14:26-27

26 But the Comforter, which is the Holy Ghost, whom the Father will send in my name, he shall teach you all things, and bring all things to your remembrance, whatsoever I have said unto you. **27** Peace I leave with you, my peace I give unto you: not as the world giveth, give I unto you. Let not your heart be troubled, neither let it be afraid. KJV

It is good to know you have a friend who sticks with you no matter how bad things get, and is still there when things are great, the Holy Spirit is a gift to you from God. When a gift is given from the heart, We should be eager recipients of the gift presented. So don't be afraid, let the peace of God flood over you.

HE IS YOUR COMFORTER.

"IN GOD WE TRUST"

Pastor Ray

JULY 2

GODS WORDS WILL PRODUCE

Isa 55:8-11

8 For my thoughts are not your thoughts, neither are your ways my ways, saith the Lord. **9** For as the heavens are higher than the earth, so are my ways higher than your ways, and my thoughts than your thoughts. **10** For as the rain cometh down, and the snow from heaven, and returneth not thither, but watereth the earth, and maketh it bring forth and bud, that it may give seed to the sower, and bread to the eater: **11** So shall my word be that goeth forth out of my mouth: it shall not return unto me void, but it shall accomplish that which I please, and it shall prosper in the thing whereto I sent it. KJV

God never misses the mark, when He says something He will stand behind His word to bring it to pass.

GOD NEVER FAILS. HAVE A GREAT DAY

"IN GOD WE TRUST"

Pastor Ray

JULY 3

LET GOD BE YOUR PARTNER

Prov 16:1-3

The preparations of the heart in man, and the answer of the tongue, is from the Lord. **2** All the ways of a man are clean in his own eyes; but the Lord weigheth the spirits. **3** Commit thy works unto the Lord, and thy thoughts shall be established. KJV

If we will let God help, we will not come up short, He knows what we need to be a success, and knows how to find it and bring it to us.

FOLLOW GOD. AND HAVE A GREAT FOURTH OF JULY WEEK END.

"IN GOD WE TRUST"

Pastor Ray

JULY 4

FAMILY RELATIONSHIPS ARE IMPORTANT TO GOD

Mal 4:2-3,5:6

2 But unto you that fear my name shall the Sun of righteousness arise with healing in his wings; and ye shall go forth, and grow up as calves of the stall. **3** And ye shall tread down the wicked; for they shall be ashes under the soles of your feet in the day that I shall do this, saith the Lord of hosts. **5** Behold, I will send you Elijah the prophet before the coming of the great and dreadful day of the Lord: **6** And he shall turn the heart of the fathers to the children, and the heart of the children to their fathers, lest I come and smite the earth with a curse. KJV

God is able to heal and correct relationships much faster than we can. Our problem is giving them to Him and then not taking them back when we, (according to our time schedule), think He has not taken care of them quick enough. Pray and give God the relationship, trusting Him to handle it on His time schedule, AND ENJOY YOUR TIME TOGETHER, remember God is dealing with people who are not always obedient to His urgings.

HAVE A HAPPY AND SAFE FOURTH OF JULY HOLIDAY.

"IN GOD WE TRUST"

JULY 5

JESUS IS OUR MAKER

John 1:1-4

In the beginning was the Word, and the Word was with God, and the Word was God. **2** The same was in the beginning with God. **3** All things were made by him; and without him was not any thing made that was made. **4** In him was life; and the life was the light of men. KJV

Nothing was made without the Word, Jesus being the Word is our maker and the producer of our life, He made us so therefore He can fix us when we are broken, we can be broken in many ways by hurts, by accidents, and ill spoken words, but He has the original design to go by in repairing us, bringing us back to the original way that He made us.

GIVE HIM A CHANCE. HAVE A GREAT HOLIDAY.

"IN GOD WE TRUST"

Pastor Ray

JULY 6

YOU ARE CROWNED WITH LOVING KINDNESS

Psalm 103:2-4

2 Bless the LORD, O my soul, and forget not all his benefits: 3 Who forgiveth all thine iniquities; who healeth all thy diseases; 4 Who redeemeth thy life from destruction; who crowneth thee with lovingkindness and tender mercies; KJV

Know that God's love never fails, and His mercy endures forever, He is our healer, our helper. He forgives our sin and forgets them and crowns us with loving kindness and tender mercies. This love of God is more powerful than anything, and it is directed at you.

DON'T HIDE FROM HIS LOVE. HAVE A GREAT DAY

"IN GOD WE TRUST"

Pastor Ray

JULY 7

GOD KNOWS YOUR HEART

Ps 7:8-9

8 The Lord shall judge the people: judge me, O Lord, according to my righteousness, and according to mine integrity that is in me. **9** Oh let the wickedness of the wicked come to an end; but establish the just: for the righteous God trieth the hearts and reins. KJV

Let God have his way with you, shaping you into the person He wants you to be, free from sin, upright before Him, examples for others to see. God wants to use us, His children to show the rest of the world how to live in His love. God wants you to live out the plan that He has for you. We are told what that is in, Jer 9:11, For I know the thoughts that I think toward you, saith the Lord, thoughts of peace, and not of evil, to give you an expected end. KJV

LET GOD LEAD YOU TO YOUR EXPECTED END, AND ENJOY THE TRIP. HAVE A GREAT DAY

"IN GOD WE TRUST"

JULY 8

WHY ME GOD?

Ps 8:4-6

4 What is man, that thou art mindful of him? and the son of man, that thou visitest him? **5** For thou hast made him a little lower than the angels, and hast crowned him with glory and honour. **6** Thou madest him to have dominion over the works of thy hands; thou hast put all things under his feet: KJV

You were on his mind before you were born, and has chosen you to be in His family, one of His children, so that He can bless you and make you successful, God our Father has it all planned out and has done His part, now it up to us to do our part, without rebellion.

WHY YOU? BECAUSE HE LOVES YOU, BASK IN HIS LOVE, AND HAVE A GREAT LIFE.

"IN GOD WE TRUST"

Pastor Ray

JULY 9

YOUR SORROW SHALL BE REMOVED

Isa 35:8-10

8 And an highway shall be there, and a way, and it shall be called The way of holiness; the unclean shall not pass over it; but it shall be for those: the wayfaring men, though fools, shall not err therein. **9** No lion shall be there, nor any ravenous beast shall go up thereon, it shall not be found there; but the redeemed shall walk there: **10** And the ransomed of the Lord shall return, and come to Zion with songs and everlasting joy upon their heads: they shall obtain joy and gladness, and sorrow and sighing shall flee away. KJV

Release your sorrow and worries to the Lord for He is willing to carry them for you and replace them with joy and gladness. His joy in you is your strength to get you through any situation. Let your sorrow go as He can do nothing with it as long as you hold onto it.

LET IT GO, AND HAVE A GREAT DAY.

"IN GOD WE TRUST"

Pastor Ray

JULY 10

DON'T GIVE UP

Gal 6:7-10

7 Be not deceived; God is not mocked: for whatsoever a man soweth, that shall he also reap. **8** For he that soweth to his flesh shall of the flesh reap corruption; but he that soweth to the Spirit shall of the Spirit reap life everlasting. **9** And let us not be weary in well doing: for in due season we shall reap, if we faint not. **10** As we have therefore opportunity, let us do good unto all men, especially unto them who are of the household of faith. KJV

This means don't give up in standing in faith, believing in God for the things you desire. Keep on loving the unlovely, helping the ungrateful, being kind to the unkind, being friendly to the unfriendly. For from what we sow, we shall reap a harvest. Sow an act of kindness for those you love.

SOW AND REAP. HAVE A NICE DAY

"IN GOD WE TRUST"

Pastor Ray

JULY 11

HELP IS AMONG YOU

Matt 18:18-20

18 Verily I say unto you, Whatsoever ye shall bind on earth shall be bound in heaven: and whatsoever ye shall loose on earth shall be loosed in heaven. **19** Again I say unto you, That if two of you shall agree on earth as touching any thing that they shall ask, it shall be done for them of my Father which is in heaven. **20** For where two or three are gathered together in my name, there am I in the midst of them. KJV

Find a prayer partner, and get in agreement with each other about what you are praying for, turn it over to God and let him handle it. He is with you with all the help you will ever need. This is a promise from God, and He always keeps His promise.

CALL ON HIM, HE WILL ANSWER. HAVE A JOYFUL DAY.

"IN GOD WE TRUST"

Pastor Ray

JULY 12

SUCCESS FOR YOUR CHILDREN

Isa 54:13-14

13 And all thy children shall be taught of the Lord; and great shall be the peace of thy children. **14** In righteousness shalt thou be established: thou shalt be far from oppression; for thou shalt not fear: and from terror; for it shall not come near thee. **17** No weapon that is formed against thee shall prosper; and every tongue that shall rise against thee in judgment thou shalt condemn. This is the heritage of the servants of the Lord, and their righteousness is of me, saith the Lord. KJV

When our children are taught of the Lord, (Have the Word of God sown in their heart), there will be peace and success for them all their lives, which gives the parent joy as they see the Word of God working in their lives. I don't think there is anyone who would not want their children to be successful, and see the whole family, including you living, under Gods protection.

IF WE DO OUR PART, GOD WILL DO HIS. HAVE A GREAT DAY.

"IN GOD WE TRUST"

Pastor Ray

JULY 13

SHARP WORDS HURT

Proverbs 21:23

23 Whoso keepeth his mouth and his tongue keepeth his soul from troubles. KJV

We should always speak or do unto others as we would have them do or speak to us. If you can't say something good, don't say anything.

LISTEN AND SAY LITTLE. HAVE A GOOD DAY.

"IN GOD WE TRUST"

Pastor Ray

JULY 14

OUR WORDS ARE PRODUCTIVE

Eph 4:29-32

29 Let no corrupt communication proceed out of your mouth, but that which is good to the use of edifying, that it may minister grace unto the hearers. **30** And grieve not the holy Spirit of God, whereby ye are sealed unto the day of redemption. **31** Let all bitterness, and wrath, and anger, and clamour, and evil speaking, be put away from you, with all malice: **32** And be ye kind one to another, tenderhearted, forgiving one another, even as God for Christ's sake hath forgiven you. KJV

Our words reflect what is in our heart. If we will fill our hearts with love and the Word of God it will affect the way we speak and live, causing us to be a blessing to those around us. Bringing peace and joy into our lives.

OPEN YOUR HEART AND RECEIVE. ENJOY YOUR DAY.

"IN GOD WE TRUST"

Pastor Ray

JULY 15

YOU ARE NEVER ALONE

Deut 20:3-4

3 And shall say unto them, Hear, O Israel, ye approach this day unto battle against your enemies: let not your hearts faint, fear not, and do not tremble, neither be ye terrified because of them; **4** For the Lord your God is he that goeth with you, to fight for you against your enemies, to save you. KJV

Put your name in the place of Israel, make this a personal message for you, and know you are never alone in the fight, you have a warrior with you that will fight for you and stand beside you until victory is yours. He will never leave you or forsake you, even when you may think He is no where around, He is still there.

FEAR NOT, GOD HAS YOUR BACK. HAVE A GREAT DAY

"IN GOD WE TRUST"

Pastor Ray

JULY 16

SEED TIME AND HARVEST, NEVER ENDS

Gal 6:7-8

7 Be not deceived; God is not mocked: for whatsoever a man soweth, that shall he also reap. **8** For he that soweth to his flesh shall of the flesh reap corruption; but he that soweth to the Spirit shall of the Spirit reap life everlasting. KJV

It is certain that we will reap a harvest on what we sow, plant or give out, Gen 8:22 in the NIV tells us "As long as the earth endures, seedtime and harvest, cold and heat, summer and winter, day and night will never cease." If we want love, we need to give it out, if we want friends, we need to be friendly. In other word, do unto others as you would have them do unto you. God gave his Son so that we could give ourselves to Him in return, so we could spend eternity with Him.

BE A GIVER, AND HAVE A GREAT DAY.

"IN GOD WE TRUST"

Pastor Ray

JULY 17

THERE IS A TIME FOR EVERYTHING
A TIME TO LOVE,
A TIME TO FORGIVE,
A TIME TO GIVE,
A TIME TO RECEIVE,

Luke 6:36-38

36 Be ye therefore merciful, as your Father also is merciful. **37** Judge not, and ye shall not be judged: condemn not, and ye shall not be condemned: forgive, and ye shall be forgiven: **38** Give, and it shall be given unto you; good measure, pressed down, and shaken together, and running over, shall men give into your bosom. For with the same measure that ye mete withal it shall be measured to you again. KJV

Our Father God is thinking about us all the time, wanting us to be as much like Him as possible. Our hearts should open to be generous, not closed to be stingy. Let's not be the judge of another's needs, but be obedient to what God would have us to do, not questioning ever time He moves on our hearts to give. Let God be a blessing to someone through you.

GIVE AND BE BLESSED, HAVE A GREAT AND JOYOUS DAY.

"IN GOD WE TRUST"

Pastor Ray

JULY 18

DON'T GIVE UP, JOY IS COMING

Ps 30:4-5

4 Sing unto the Lord, O ye saints of his, and give thanks at the remembrance of his holiness. **5** For his anger endureth but a moment; in his favour is life: weeping may endure for a night, but joy cometh in the morning. KJV

You are loved, and cared for, in His sight you are beautiful and precious. His desire for you is to be full of life and joy. His joy is your strength, and the fruit of His Spirit is your life, in all your ways acknowledge Him and He will direct and protect you.

RELAX IN HIS LOVE, AND HAVE A GREAT AND JOYFUL DAY.

"IN GOD WE TRUST"

Pastor Ray

JULY 19

DO YOU NEED COMFORTING?

John 14:26-27

26 But the Comforter, which is the Holy Ghost, whom the Father will send in my name, he shall teach you all things, and bring all things to your remembrance, whatsoever I have said unto you.**27** Peace I leave with you, my peace I give unto you: not as the world giveth, give I unto you. Let not your heart be troubled, neither let it be afraid. KJV

When you need comforting, open your heart and mind to the helping hand of the Holy Spirit of God, for He has already been sent to help, if you will let Him. The choice is yours, receive Him and let Him help, then let the peace of God flood over you, knowing that every thing is going to be all right.

DON'T BE AFRAID, TRUST GOD, AND HAVE A GREAT DAY.

"IN GOD WE TRUST"

JULY 20

YOUTH AND AGE BOTH HAVE HONOR

Prov 20:29

29 The glory of young men is their strength: and the beauty of old men is the gray head. KJV

In our youth we strive to display our health and vigor, and in our mature years we display our wisdom, and yet we go to each other for help, youth to the older for help with what they do not understand, and the aged to the youth for help with things they can no longer do.

WE NEED EACH OTHER. LOVE AND HAVE A GREAT DAY

"IN GOD WE TRUST"

JULY 21

YOU HAVE SOMEONE WHO CARES

Isa 54:9-10

9 For this is as the waters of Noah unto me: for as I have sworn that the waters of Noah should no more go over the earth; so have I sworn that I would not be wroth with thee, nor rebuke thee. **10** For the mountains shall depart, and the hills be removed; but my kindness shall not depart from thee, neither shall the covenant of my peace be removed, saith the Lord that hath mercy on thee.

KJV

God's Word is true, when He says something He means it. When He makes a promise you know that He will keep it. His kindness will not be taken from you, He will remain loyal to you, and His mercy will remain on you. Trust Him. For He truly cares about you.

GOD IS NOT MAD AT YOU. HAVE A LOVELY DAY

"IN GOD WE TRUST"

Pastor Ray

JULY 22

TIRED OF THE STRUGGLE?

Matt 11:28-30

28 Come unto me, all ye that labour and are heavy laden, and I will give you rest. **29** Take my yoke upon you, and learn of me; for I am meek and lowly in heart: and ye shall find rest unto your souls. **30** For my yoke is easy, and my burden is light. KJV

God does not ask us to do anything other than come to Him just as we are, tired and worn out from the every day struggle of life, the job, the kids, or just everything in general, but with an open heart willing to receive, and He will give us rest, peace and assurance in our hearts that everything is going to be all right.

BELIEVE AND RECEIVE, HAVE A GREAT DAY.

"IN GOD WE TRUST"

Pastor Ray

JULY 23

NEVER GIVE UP

Heb 10:32-36

32 But call to remembrance the former days, in which, after ye were illuminated, ye endured a great fight of afflictions; **33** Partly, whilst ye were made a gazingstock both by reproaches and afflictions; and partly, whilst ye became companions of them that were so used. **34** For ye had compassion of me in my bonds, and took joyfully the spoiling of your goods, knowing in yourselves that ye have in heaven a better and an enduring substance. **35** Cast not away therefore your confidence, which hath great recompence of reward. **36** For ye have need of patience, that, after ye have done the will of God, ye might receive the promise. KJV

By keeping our confidence in God, He can keep His confidence in us. In other words He will be able to trust us with the reward we receive. Our obedience to Him is better than sacrifice.

STAND FAST AND RECEIVE THE PROMISE, HAVE A GREAT DAY

"IN GOD WE TRUST"

Pastor Ray

JULY 24

YOU CAN HAVE A GOOD LIFE

John 15:1-4

I am the true vine, and my Father is the husbandman. **2** Every branch in me that beareth not fruit he taketh away: and every branch that beareth fruit, he purgeth it, that it may bring forth more fruit. **3** Now ye are clean through the word which I have spoken unto you. **4** Abide in me, and I in you. As the branch cannot bear fruit of itself, except it abide in the vine; no more can ye, except ye abide in me. KJV

God is looking out for us, to protect, guide, and help us through the rough times we get ourselves into, but if we will walk and talk with Jesus we will be able to stay on the right path and out of trouble, and he will send the Holy Spirit to comfort us, and give us the strength to endure to the finish line.

WALK IN VICTORY, AND HAVE A GREAT DAY

"IN GOD WE TRUST"

Pastor Ray

JULY 25

GOD HEALS YOUR BROKEN HEART

Ps 147:3-6

3 He healeth the broken in heart, and bindeth up their wounds. **4** He telleth the number of the stars; he calleth them all by their names. **5** Great is our Lord, and of great power: his understanding is infinite. **6** The Lord lifteth up the meek: he casteth the wicked down to the ground. KJV

God knows you better than you know yourself, He loves you and cares for you. When your heart aches so does His. Scripture tells us that He stands at the door (of our hearts) and knocks. If we will open the door He will come in and heal our broken hearts, and soothe our wounds, lift us up, and put us on our feet again.

GIVE HIM A CHANCE. AND HAVE A GREAT AND PROSPEROUS DAY.

"IN GOD WE TRUST"

Pastor Ray

JULY 26

ARISE AND SHINE, YOUR LIGHT IS COME

Isa 60:1-2

Arise, shine; for thy light is come, and the glory of the Lord is risen upon thee. **2** For, behold, the darkness shall cover the earth, and gross darkness the people: but the Lord shall arise upon thee, and his glory shall be seen upon thee. KJV

Isa 60:1-2

1 ARISE [from the depression and prostration in which circumstances have kept you—rise to a new life]! Shine (be radiant with the glory of the Lord), for your light has come, and the glory of the Lord has risen upon you! **2** For behold, darkness shall cover the earth, and dense darkness [all] peoples, but the Lord shall arise upon you, and His glory shall be seen on you. AMP

Not only does God tell us to arise and shine, He also tells us what makes us shine. For the Glory of the Lord is risen upon you. This brightness is Jesus shining out of you, for He is the Light for all to see.

STAND IN HIS BRIGHTNESS, HAVE A GREAT DAY.

"IN GOD WE TRUST"

Pastor Ray

JULY 27

FEAR NOT: HELP IS ON THE WAY

Isa 35:3-4

3 Strengthen the weak hands and make firm the feeble *and* tottering knees. **4** Say to those who are of a fearful *and* hasty heart, Be strong, fear not! Behold, your God will come with vengeance; with the recompense of God He will come and save you. AMP

It is good to know that God is never late and never misses the target, even though we may think He does, but He knows us better than we know ourselves and knows when and what kind of help we need and is ready to supply it, all we have to do is humble ourselves, ask Him in prayer, and He will hear and respond.

ASK, BELIEVE, AND RECEIVE. HAVE A NICE DAY.

"IN GOD WE TRUST"

Pastor Ray

JULY 28

GOD WILL DO MIRACLES FOR YOU

Isa 35:5-7

5 Then the eyes of the blind shall be opened, and the ears of the deaf shall be unstopped. **6** Then shall the lame man leap as an hart, and the tongue of the dumb sing: for in the wilderness shall waters break out, and streams in the desert. **7** And the parched ground shall become a pool, and the thirsty land springs of water: in the habitation of dragons, where each lay, shall be grass with reeds and rushes. KJV

God's love for you is so strong, and His trust in you so high, that *He will do all these things for you*, and then give you the power to transfer these gifts to others in the name of Jesus. *God will do miracles for you and through you.*

GIVE HIM A CHANCE. HAVE A GREAT DAY.

"IN GOD WE TRUST"

JULY 30

CHEER UP YOU ARE NOT ALONE

Deuteronomy 31:6

6 Be strong and of a good courage, fear not, nor be afraid of them: for the LORD thy God, he it is that doth go with thee; he will not fail thee, nor forsake thee. KJV

God is not only with you, He goes out ahead of you to prepare the way that you will find favor. Don't let fear steal your victory.

STAY WITH GOD, AND HAVE A GREAT DAY.

"IN GOD WE TRUST"

JULY 31

GOD HAS A HIDING PLACE FOR YOU

Ps 31:19-20

19 Oh how great is thy goodness, which thou hast laid up for them that fear thee; which thou hast wrought for them that trust in thee before the sons of men! **20** Thou shalt hide them in the secret of thy presence from the pride of man: thou shalt keep them secretly in a pavilion from the strife of tongues. KJV

God has a hiding place for all that love Him and turn to Him in their time of trouble, Don't be shy, ask Him for help, run into His arms for protection, for His love for you is everlasting.

LOVE AND TRUST HIM. HAVE A GREAT AND PEACEFUL DAY.

"IN GOD WE TRUST"

Pastor Ray

AUGUST 1

DO YOU HAVE A PROBLEM? GOD IS ABLE TO HANDLE IT

Mark 10:23-27

23 And Jesus looked round about, and saith unto his disciples, How hardly shall they that have riches enter into the kingdom of God! **24** And the disciples were astonished at his words. But Jesus answereth again, and saith unto them, Children, how hard is it for them that trust in riches to enter into the kingdom of God! **25** It is easier for a camel to go through the eye of a needle, than for a rich man to enter into the kingdom of God. **26** And they were astonished out of measure, saying among themselves, Who then can be saved? **27** And Jesus looking upon them saith, With men it is impossible, but not with God: for with God all things are possible. KJV

Gods desire is to help us through every situation no matter how bad it may look. He gives Christ to strengthen us, and the Holy Spirit to comfort and help us, He assures us that nothing is impossible for Him, and in Him we can do all things even when it looks impossible, if we will only believe and trust Him. Give Him the problem and leave it with Him to work with. Don't take it back after a few minutes, give Him some time, remember He is working with people.

TRUSTING JESUS IS YOUR KEY. HAVE A GREAT DAY.

"IN GOD WE TRUST"

Pastor Ray

AUGUST 2

LET GOD KNOW YOUR NEEDS

Phil 4:4-7

4 Rejoice in the Lord alway: and again I say, Rejoice. **5** Let your moderation be known unto all men. The Lord is at hand. **6** Be careful for nothing; but in every thing by prayer and supplication with thanksgiving let your requests be made known unto God. **7** And the peace of God, which passeth all understanding, shall keep your hearts and minds through Christ Jesus. KJV

Phil 4:4-7

4 Always be full of joy in the Lord. I say it again—rejoice! **5** Let everyone see that you are considerate in all you do. Remember, the Lord is coming soon. **6** Don't worry about anything; instead, pray about everything. Tell God what you need, and thank him for all he has done. **7** Then you will experience God's peace, which exceeds anything we can understand. His peace will guard your hearts and minds as you live in Christ Jesus. NLT

Let us make our needs known to God, knowing that our prayers are heard as we lift our voices to Him. And while we are praying let us also pray for our nation, state, city and our leaders in all areas, pray for our schools and churches, also our friends, neighbors, families, and coworkers, also our troops and that victory over our enemies will come quickly, also for harmony and agreement in Washington, to lead our country back to the position that God intended it to be.

LET ALL PEOPLE CALLED BY HIS NAME PRAY, HAVE A GREAT DAY

"IN GOD WE TRUST"

Pastor Ray

AUGUST 3

DO YOU WANT A GOOD LIFE?

Prov 3:1-2

My son, do not forget my teaching, but keep my commands in your heart, **2** for they will prolong your life many years and bring you prosperity. NIV

God gives us instructions on how to live a good life, He tells us in His word that the way of a transgressor is hard, but do we believe? No, we have to go out and get in trouble and prove to ourselves that the way of a transgressor is hard, instead of taking God at His Word.

FOLLOW GOD'S INSTRUCTIONS AND HAVE A GOOD AND PROSPEROUS LIFE

"IN GOD WE TRUST"

Pastor Ray

AUGUST 4

GOD IS NEVER LATE

Deuteronomy 28:12-13

12 The LORD shall open unto thee his good treasure, the heaven to give the rain unto thy land in his season, and to bless all the work of thine hand: and thou shalt lend unto many nations, and thou shalt not borrow. 13 And the LORD shall make thee the head, and not the tail; and thou shalt be above only, and thou shalt not be beneath; if that thou hearken unto the commandments of the LORD thy God, which I command thee this day, to observe and to do them: KJV

God is never late, He will always send his provisions on time, and He will give you a helping hand to get you through your rough times, even though we may not think so. Our part is to hear Him and obey His commandments.

PRAY & OBEY, HAVE A GREAT DAY

"IN GOD WE TRUST"

Pastor Ray

AUGUST 5

GOD PICKED YOU

John 15:15-17

15 Henceforth I call you not servants; for the servant knoweth not what his lord doeth: but I have called you friends; for all things that I have heard of my Father I have made known unto you. **16** Ye have not chosen me, but I have chosen you, and ordained you, that ye should go and bring forth fruit, and that your fruit should remain: that whatsoever ye shall ask of the Father in my name, he may give it you. **17** These things I command you, that ye love one another. KJV

God has chosen you out of His love for you, that of all people you could be the recipient of his blessings. He also instructed you how to get in position to receive and, produce the fruit of the Holy Spirit, and love one another.

LET GOD BE YOUR FRIEND, HAVE A GREAT DAY

"IN GOD WE TRUST"

Pastor Ray

AUGUST 6

GOD HEARS YOUR PRAYERS

Ps 6:8-10

8 Depart from me, all ye workers of iniquity; for the Lord hath heard the voice of my weeping. **9** The Lord hath heard my supplication; the Lord will receive my prayer. **10** Let all mine enemies be ashamed and sore vexed: let them return and be ashamed suddenly. KJV

God's ears are tuned to your prayers, and He knows your heart, and needs. Our part is to ask in faith, believing that He has heard us and is handling our requests, and then thank Him in every prayer for your answer. Don't take your problem back, leave it with Him, let Him take care of it, and be thankful that He is on your side.

PRAY AND LISTEN. HAVE A GREAT DAY.

"IN GOD WE TRUST"

Pastor Ray

AUGUST 7

LIVE GODS WAY AND BE HAPPY

Prov 7:1-3

My son, keep my words, and lay up my commandments with thee. **2** Keep my commandments, and live; and my law as the apple of thine eye. **3** Bind them upon thy fingers, write them upon the table of thine heart. KJV

when we keep God's commandments, and have His Word stored in our hearts, then we can expect to live a good and prosperous life worth living.

KEEP GOD'S WORDS IN YOUR HEART. HAVE A GREAT DAY.

"IN GOD WE TRUST"

Pastor Ray

AUGUST 8

KINDNESS AND PEACE IS YOUR TO KEEP

Isaiah 54:10

10 For the mountains shall depart, and the hills be removed; but my kindness shall not depart from thee, neither shall the covenant of my peace be removed, saith the LORD that hath mercy on thee. KJV

Isa 54:10

10 For though the mountains should depart and the hills be shaken *or* removed, yet My love *and* kindness shall not depart from you, nor shall My covenant of peace *and* completeness be removed, says the Lord, Who has compassion on you. AMP

God's Word is true, when He says something He means it. When He makes a promise you know that He will keep it. His kindness will not be taken from you, He will remain loyal to you, and His mercy and peace will remain on you.

HAVE FAITH IN GOD. AND HAVE A GREAT DAY.

"IN GOD WE TRUST"

AUGUST 9

NEVER GIVE UP YOUR CONFIDENCE!

Hebrews 10:35-36

35 Cast not away therefore your confidence, which hath great recompence of reward. 36 For ye have need of patience, that, after ye have done the will of God, ye might receive the promise. KJV

Heb 10:35-36

35 Do not, therefore, fling away your fearless confidence, for it carries a great *and* glorious compensation of reward. **36** For you have need of steadfast patience *and* endurance, so that you may perform *and* fully accomplish the will of God, and thus receive *and* carry away [and enjoy to the full] what is promised. AMP

By keeping our confidence in God, He can keep His confidence in us. In other words He will be able to trust us with the reward we receive.

JESUS WOULD NEVER TELL US TO DO SOMETHING THAT WE COULD NOT DO. OBEY AND HAVE A GREAT DAY.

"IN GOD WE TRUST"

AUGUST 10

THE COMFORTER HAS COME

John 14:26

But the Comforter, which is the Holy Ghost, whom the Father will send in my name, he shall teach you all things, and bring all things to your remembrance, whatsoever I have said unto you. KJV

When you need comforting, open your heart and mind to the helping hand of the Holy Spirit, for He has been sent to help, if you will let Him. The choice is yours, receive Him and let the peace of God flood over you, that you know every thing will be okay.

GOD IS STILL WITH YOU, AND KEEPING HIS PROMISES. EVERY THING IS GOING TO BE ALL RIGHT.

"IN GOD WE TRUST"

Pastor Ray

AUGUST 11

GOD HAS SPECIAL PLANS FOR YOU

Jer 1:5

5 Before I formed you in the womb I knew [and] approved of you [as My chosen instrument], and before you were born I separated *and* set you apart, consecrating you; [and] I appointed you as a prophet to the nations. AMP

God not only knows you, He has great plans for you, He knew you before you were conceived, and knows where you are going and what you are doing, he wants you to be with Him here and now, and throughout eternity, that's a long time to put up with us, and yet He will not force us to do anything we do not want to do. God has promised never to leave us or forsake us, and He always keeps His promises, and expect us to do our part so He can do His. The *choice is ours.*

WALK WITH GOD, AND ENJOY THE JOURNEY. HAVE A GREAT DAY.

"IN GOD WE TRUST"

Pastor Ray

AUGUST 12

LET GOD KNOW YOUR DESIRE

Philippians 4:6-7

6 Be careful for nothing; but in every thing by prayer and supplication with thanksgiving let your requests be made known unto God. 7 And the peace of God, which passeth all understanding, shall keep your hearts and minds through Christ Jesus. KJV

Phil 4:6-7

6 Do not fret *or* have any anxiety about anything, but in every circumstance *and* in everything, by prayer and petition (definite requests), with thanksgiving, continue to make your wants known to God. **7** And God's peace [shall be yours, that tranquil state of a soul assured of its salvation through Christ, and so fearing nothing from God and being content with its earthly lot of whatever sort that is, that peace] which transcends all understanding shall garrison *and* mount guard over your hearts and minds in Christ Jesus. AMP

By talking to God in prayer with a thankful heart, and loving Him as a Son loves his Father, and letting Him know your hearts desires, you can have peace beyond what you could possibly expect. Peace is just one of the gifts the Father loves to give His children. Look forward to His gifts with joy, just like you did when you were a child waiting for the big gift you were promised.

GOD IS FAITHFUL TO KEEP HIS PROMISES. HAVE A GREAT DAY.

"IN GOD WE TRUST"

AUGUST 13

LET GOD SEE YOU THROUGH

Ephesians 6:10-11

10 Finally, my brethren, be strong in the Lord, and in the power of his might. 11 Put on the whole armor of God, that ye may be able to stand against the wiles of the devil. KJV

Eph 6:10-11

10 In conclusion, be strong in the Lord [be empowered through your union with Him]; draw your strength from Him [that strength which His boundless might provides]. **11** Put on God's whole armor [the armor of a heavy-armed soldier which God supplies], that you may be able successfully to stand up against [all] the strategies *and* the deceits of the devil. AMP

When All Mighty God is standing behind you, there is no power on earth that can stand against you and Him. And when you are dressed in God's armor, the Devil will run from you. Why? Because when you are fully dressed in God's armor and close the face plate on your helmet, he has no way of knowing who is in there and he has been whipped once by the guy wearing that armor and does not want to be whipped again.

GET DRESSED, CLOSE THE FACE PLATE, AND HAVE A SAFE AND HAPPY DAY WALKING WITH GOD.

"IN GOD WE TRUST"

AUGUST 14

WHY ME GOD?

John 15:16

16 Ye have not chosen me, but I have chosen you, and ordained you, that ye should go and bring forth fruit, and that your fruit should remain: that whatsoever ye shall ask of the Father in my name, he may give it you. KJV

God has picked you out of the crowd, to shower you with gifts, to spend time with you, to protect you and keep you safe, so that people will see in you the love of God that He has for His chosen ones. You may ask, why?

BECAUSE HE LOVES YOU, AND PLANNED FOR YOU.

Jer 29:11-12

For I know the plans I have for you," declares the Lord, "plans to prosper you and not to harm you, plans to give you hope and a future. NIV

RELAX, LET GOD HAVE HIS WAY WITH YOU. HIS IS PURE LOVE, NEVER ENDING.

"IN GOD WE TRUST"

AUGUST 15

THERE IS WARFARE GOING ON

Ephesians 6:12-13

12 For we wrestle not against flesh and blood, but against principalities, against powers, against the rulers of the darkness of this world, against spiritual wickedness in high places. 13 Wherefore take unto you the whole armour of God, that ye may be able to withstand in the evil day, and having done all, to stand. KJV

Don't forget even one piece of God's armor. You would not go to work wearing only one shoe, or a half of a coat, a tie with no shirt. So don't leave home without the full armor of God, when you are fully clothed in God's armor, the enemy cannot touch you. Isn't it great to know that in Jesus you have the victory, for He has forgiven all of your sins, and paid the price for your healing, and will fight all your battles, (2 Chron 20:15 b. Do not be afraid! Don't be discouraged by this mighty army, for the battle is not yours, but God's. NLT)

LET GOD LEAD YOU TO VICTORY. HAVE A GREAT DAY

"IN GOD WE TRUST"

Pastor Ray

AUGUST 16

GOD IS WAITING FOR YOU

Deut 4:29-31

29 But if from thence thou shalt seek the Lord thy God, thou shalt find him, if thou seek him with all thy heart and with all thy soul. **30** When thou art in tribulation, and all these things are come upon thee, even in the latter days, if thou turn to the Lord thy God, and shalt be obedient unto his voice; **31** (For the Lord thy God is a merciful God;) he will not forsake thee, neither destroy thee, nor forget the covenant of thy fathers which he sware unto them. KJV

When hard times come, run to God, as hard as you can, don't run from Him. He promised long ago that He would be merciful, if we would search for Him and return to Him and that He would not forsake us. Know that He is with you always, even when you don't feel like He is. He waits for you to come to Him.

CATCH GOD, HE IS WAITING FOR YOU, THEN PRAY AND LISTEN, HAVE A GREAT DAY.

"IN GOD WE TRUST"

Pastor Ray

AUGUST 17

LET YOUR HEART BE MERRY

Proverbs 17:22

22 A merry heart doeth good like a medicine: but a broken spirit drieth the bones.

The King James Version, (Cambridge: Cambridge) 1769.

Laugh and the world laughs with you, so they say. God says a merry heart is like a medicine to you, it makes you feel good, and fills you with joy and causes those around you to rejoice with you.

LET JESUS BRING JOY TO YOU TODAY, HAVE A GREAT AND JOYFUL DAY.

"IN GOD WE TRUST"

Pastor Ray

AUGUST 18

LAUGHTER MAKES THE HEART JOYOUS

Ps 118:22-24

22 The stone which the builders refused is become the head stone of the corner.**23** This is the Lord's doing; it is marvellous in our eyes. **24** This is the day which the Lord hath made; we will rejoice and be glad in it. KJV

No matter what we may face on this day, it is still the day the Lord has made and we are to rejoice and be glad in it. When we rejoice God hears and will join with us and see to it that we get through the day in victory. And when we have a day of victory, we are glad in it, and when we are glad we get tickled, and when we are tickled we laugh, that is when God joins in and laughs with us, filling our hearts with His joy which is our strength.

LAUGH A LOT, AND LET GOD COME INTO YOUR LIFE, HAVE A GREAT DAY.

"IN GOD WE TRUST"

Pastor Ray

AUGUST 19

YOUR ARE BEAUTIFUL IN GODS EYES

2 Corinthians 5:17

17 Therefore if any man be in Christ, he is a new creature: old things are passed away; behold, all things are become new.

The King James Version, (Cambridge: Cambridge) 1769.

Did you ever hear the song, This old House? Or see someone buy an old house to fix up. That person doesn't see the house as it is, but as it will be when he is finished with it. God is the same with us, He takes us just the way we are, then proceeds to change us into the finished product that only He can see, a beautiful creature created in His Image. A fit dwelling place for Him to come and make His Home.

YOU ARE BEAUTIFUL IN GOD'S EYES. HAVE A GREAT DAY

"IN GOD WE TRUST"

Pastor Ray

AUGUST 20

DOES IT SEEM LIKE THERE IS NEVER ENOUGH?

Prov 3:5, 3:9-10

5 Trust in the Lord with all thine heart; and lean not unto thine own understanding. **9** Honour the Lord with thy substance, and with the firstfruits of all thine increase: **10** So shall thy barns be filled with plenty, and thy presses shall burst out with new wine. KJV

God promises that if we will honor Him. Put Him first place in our lives, that He will put us first place with Him, and see to it that we are well supplied in every area to over flowing, having more than enough, and plenty to share with others.

LET GOD SHOW YOU THE WAY, TRUST HIM. HAVE A GREAT DAY

"IN GOD WE TRUST"

Pastor Ray

AUGUST 21

GOD'S LOVE THROUGH US

1 John 3:16-18

16 Hereby perceive we the love of God, because he laid down his life for us: and we ought to lay down our lives for the brethren. 17 But whoso hath this worlds good, and seeth his brother have need, and shutteth up his bowels of compassion from him, how dwelleth the love of God in him? 18 My little children, let us not love in word, neither in tongue; but in deed and in truth. KJV

As we go through the day we are afforded many opportunities to show the love of God flowing through us. As we see a person in need we can stop and help or ignore the situation. We can say I love you, but do nothing, so what good have we done and what have we gained? Awhile back I stopped to help a neighbor. My cost was just a few minutes of my time, his response was great gratitude, and my reward is a new friend. The need you see could be many things, loneliness, money, physical help, etc. When we see or know a need, don't ignore God's call to your heart to help. Your reward will be great.

GIVE AND IT SHALL BE GIVEN TO YOU, WHAT YOU SOW IS WHAT YOU REAP. HAVE A GREAT DAY.

"IN GOD WE TRUST"

AUGUST 22

LET THE PEACE OF GOD KEEP YOUR HEART

Philippians 4:6-7

6 Be careful for nothing; but in every thing by prayer and supplication with thanksgiving let your requests be made known unto God. 7 And the peace of God, which passeth all understanding, shall keep your hearts and minds through Christ Jesus. KJV

Phil 4:6-7

6 Do not fret *or* have any anxiety about anything, but in every circumstance *and* in everything, by prayer and petition (definite requests), with thanksgiving, continue to make your wants known to God. **7** And God's peace [shall be yours, that tranquil state of a soul assured of its salvation through Christ, and so fearing nothing from God and being content with its earthly lot of whatever sort that is, that peace] which transcends all understanding shall garrison *and* mount guard over your hearts and minds in Christ Jesus. AMP

God has already made provisions for you to have His peace. Your part is to go to Him in prayer with thanksgiving in your hearts, and faith in Him that He is able and willing to grant your request. He loves you as a father, for He has chosen you to be in His family. His child translated into the kingdom of His dear Son, and wants you to let His peace keep your heart and mind. His love for you is unconditional, and He is no respecter of persons.

GOD LOVES YOU, AND WANTS YOU, LET HIM HAVE HIS WAY. HAVE A GREAT DAY.

"IN GOD WE TRUST"

AUGUST 23

YOUR ARE LOVED ETERNALLY

Psalm 100:3-5

3 Know ye that the LORD he is God: it is he that hath made us, and not we ourselves; we are his people, and the sheep of his pasture. 4 Enter into his gates with thanksgiving, and into his courts with praise: be thankful unto him, and bless his name. 5 For the LORD is good; his mercy is everlasting; and his truth endureth to all generations. KJV

I am very thankful today that God's mercy endures forever. He waited fifty years for me to wake up and know who He is. That was 37 years ago, and I am still thankful for the peace that He gives me in all situations. Especially these last five years since my wife of 62 years went home to be with the Lord.

GOD IS GOOD ALL THE TIME, LET HIM BE GOOD TO YOU. HAVE A GREAT DAY.

"IN GOD WE TRUST"

AUGUST 24

YOU ARE VERY SPECIAL AND CHOSEN OF GOD

John 15:16

16 Ye have not chosen me, but I have chosen you, and ordained you, that ye should go and bring forth fruit, and that your fruit should remain: that whatsoever ye shall ask of the Father in my name, he may give it you.

The King James Version, (Cambridge: Cambridge) 1769.

Jesus has chosen you because He loves you to much to leave you the way you are. He will constantly mold and shape you into the person He wants you to be, and when you get there He has given you the power to use His name to ask and receive of the Father.

LET HIS PLAN FOR YOU BE COMPLETED. HAVE A GREAT AND PROSPEROUS DAY.

"IN GOD WE TRUST"

Pastor Ray

AUGUST 25

YOU ARE MORE THAN CONQUERORS

Romans 8:35-37

35 Who shall separate us from the love of Christ? shall tribulation, or distress, or persecution, or famine, or nakedness, or peril, or sword? 36 As it is written, For thy sake we are killed all the day long; we are accounted as sheep for the slaughter. 37 Nay, in all these things we are more than conquerors through him that loved us. KJV

In Jesus we have the victory. We should do everything in our power to stay hooked up with Him, being aware that the trials and tribulations that we get ourselves into can separate us from His love, but only if we allow it to happen. Remember, Jesus still loves you.

DON'T GIVE UP, WALK WITH JESUS, AND HAVE A PEACEFUL HAPPY DAY.

"IN GOD WE TRUST"

Pastor Ray

AUGUST 26

NOTHING IS IMPOSSIBLE FOR GOD

Luke 1:26-38

26 In the sixth month of Elizabeths pregnancy, God sent the angel Gabriel to Nazareth, a village in Galilee, 27 to a virgin named Mary. She was engaged to be married to a man named Joseph, a descendant of King David. 28 Gabriel appeared to her and said, Greetings, favored woman! The Lord is with you! 29 Confused and disturbed, Mary tried to think what the angel could mean. 30 Dont be frightened, Mary, the angel told her, for God has decided to bless you! 31 You will become pregnant and have a son, and you are to name him Jesus. 32 He will be very great and will be called the Son of the Most High. And the Lord God will give him the throne of his ancestor David. 33 And he will reign over Israel forever; his Kingdom will never end! 34 Mary asked the angel, But how can I have a baby? I am a virgin. 35 The angel replied, The Holy Spirit will come upon you, and the power of the Most High will overshadow you. So the baby born to you will be holy, and he will be called the Son of God. 36 Whats more, your relative Elizabeth has become pregnant in her old age! People used to say she was barren, but shes already in her sixth month. 37 For nothing is impossible with God. 38 Mary responded, I am the Lords servant, and I am willing to accept whatever he wants. May everything you have said come true. And then the angel left.

Holy Bible, New Living Translation, (Wheaton, IL: Tyndale House Publishers, Inc.) 1996.

This is part of God's plan to reconcile to Himself His world and mankind which He created to be his friends, to walk with Him and have fellowship with Him throughout eternity. Mary heard the words of the angel, believed the words of the angel, conceived the words of the angle and brought forth the son of God, Jesus.

MARY HEARD GOD'S WORD, BELIEVED IT, AND CONCEIVED GOD'S WORD, AND BROUGHT FORTH A SON, JESUS.

BE A BELIEVER, HAVE A GREAT DAY.

"IN GOD WE TRUST"

AUGUST 27

LONG LIFE AND PEACE

Proverbs 3:1-2

My son, forget not my law; but let thine heart keep my commandments: 2 For length of days, and long life, and peace, shall they add to thee. KJV

Prov 3:1-2

1 MY SON, forget not my law *or* teaching, but let your heart keep my commandments; **2** For length of days and years of a life [worth living] and tranquility [inward and outward and continuing through old age till death], these shall they add to you. AMP

If we do our part, God is faithful to do His part, give us length of days, a long life worth living, and peace beyond our wildest dreams. If we keep His law, and obey His commandments.

DO YOUR PART AND LET GOD BLESS YOU. HAVE A GREAT DAY

"IN GOD WE TRUST"

Pastor Ray

AUGUST 28

GOD NEVER FAILS

Heb 13:5

5 Let your character *or* moral disposition be free from love of money [including greed, avarice, lust, and craving for earthly possessions] and be satisfied with your present [circumstances and with what you have]; for He [God] Himself has said, I will not in any way fail you *nor* give you up *nor* leave you without support. [I will] not, [I will] not, [I will] not in any degree leave you helpless *nor* forsake *nor* let [you] down (relax My hold on you)! [Assuredly not!] AMP

This has been a very encouraging scripture for me There have been times when I cried out to Him and it seemed that I was getting no answer, but He was there with me, and I had to be still and know that he was God before I could hear Him. We were on a trip in The Motor home and it was acting up and I had developed a rash that would not go away, I had asked God For wisdom as I did not know what was wrong with the Motor Home, or what to do for the rash. When I got quite enough to hear, God lead me to a Evangelist friend who is a good mechanic and He fixed the motor home, and God took care of the rash and the rest of the trip went great, praise God, He is with you and will show you what to do, if you will ask then be still and listen.

PRAY, LISTEN, AND OBEY. HAVE A GREAT DAY

"IN GOD WE TRUST"

Pastor Ray

AUGUST 29

GOD HAS A SPECIAL PLACE FOR YOU

John 14:1-4

1 Let not your heart be troubled: ye believe in God, believe also in me. **2** In my Father's house are many mansions: if it were not so, I would have told you. I go to prepare a place for you.**3** And if I go and prepare a place for you, I will come again, and receive you unto myself; that where I am, there ye may be also. **4** And whither I go ye know, and the way ye know. KJV

Gods love for you is never ending, He desires for you to be with Him always, and has a dwelling place prepared for you in His house, as His hearts desire is to spend quality time with you now and through out eternity. These scriptures tells you that you know the way Jesus is going,

THE CHOICE TO FOLLOW JESUS IS UP TO YOU. HAVE A GREAT DAY.

"IN GOD WE TRUST"

Pastor Ray

AUGUST 30

GOD HAS PLANS FOR YOU

3 John 2, Jer 29:11

2 Beloved, I pray that you may prosper in all things and be in health, just as your soul prospers. 11 For I know the thoughts that I think toward you, saith the Lord, thoughts of peace, and not of evil, to give you an expected end. KJV

This is the wish of God for His children, those that believe in Him, have received Him and been translated into the kingdom of His dear Son. His plan for you is good health and prosperity in everything you do.

BELIEVE AND RECEIVE THE GIFTS OF GOD. HAVE A GREAT DAY.

"IN GOD WE TRUST"

Pastor Ray

AUGUST 31

GOD IS ON YOUR SIDE

Rom 8:31-32

31 What shall we then say to these things? If God be for us, who can be against us? **32** He that spared not his own Son, but delivered him up for us all, how shall he not with him also freely give us all things? KJV

Rom 8:31-32

31 What then shall we say to [all] this? If God is for us, who [can be] against us? [Who can be our foe, if God is on our side? **32** He who did not withhold *or* spare [even] His own Son but gave Him up for us all, will He not also with Him freely *and* graciously give us all [other] things? AMP

God is on our side and we have an army of His angels around us to see that we are protected. Our part is to enter into His rest and know that God means what He says, have faith in Him, and know He stands behind His Word, and is able to perform it.

LET GOD BE YOUR PARTNER & HELPER. HAVE A GREAT DAY.

"IN GOD WE TRUST"

Pastor Ray

SEPTEMBER 1

GOD LIKES YOU

Ps 1:1-3

1 Blessed is the man that walketh not in the counsel of the ungodly, nor standeth in the way of sinners, nor sitteth in the seat of the scornful. **2** But his delight is in the law of the Lord; and in his law doth he meditate day and night. **3** And he shall be like a tree planted by the rivers of water, that bringeth forth his fruit in his season; his leaf also shall not wither; and whatsoever he doeth shall prosper. KJV

God not only likes you, He loves you as well, and has made provisions for you to be successful, but it is up to you to accept those provisions and act on them.

STUDY HIS WORD, WALK TALL AND TRUE BEFORE GOD AND MAN, AND BE BLESSED

HAVE A WONDERFUL DAY.

"IN GOD WE TRUST"

Pastor Ray

SEPTEMBER 2

YOUR REVERENCE OF GOD BRINGS KNOWLEDGE

Prov 2:1-5

2 My son, if thou wilt receive my words, and hide my commandments with thee; **2** So that thou incline thine ear unto wisdom, and apply thine heart to understanding; **3** Yea, if thou criest after knowledge, and liftest up thy voice for understanding; **4** If thou seekest her as silver, and searchest for her as for hid treasures; **5** Then shalt thou understand the fear of the Lord, and find the knowledge of God. KJV

Prov 2:1-5

Be persistent in your pursuit of a relationship with Jesus. Open your heart and let Him come in and show you the perfect way into His wisdom and knowledge.

SEEK FIRST THE KINGDOM GOD AND HIS RIGHTEOUSNESS, AND HAVE A VERY GOOD DAY

"IN GOD WE TRUST"

SEPTEMBER 3

DON'T BE AFRAID

Prov 3:24-26

24 When thou liest down, thou shalt not be afraid: yea, thou shalt lie down, and thy sleep shall be sweet. **25** Be not afraid of sudden fear, neither of the desolation of the wicked, when it cometh. **26** For the Lord shall be thy confidence, and shall keep thy foot from being taken. KJV

This is God's promise for you, so have no fear of not waking up, enjoy your nap, have a good nights sleep, looking forward to what God has in store for you, for He is going to keep you safe and secure, as long as we allow Him to lead. We can pull away from Him any time and stop the blessing, the choice is ours,

REJOICE: YOUR WAY IS SECURE, DON'T LET WORRY STEAL JOY. HAVE A GREAT DAY.

"IN GOD WE TRUST"

Pastor Ray

SEPTEMBER 4

GOD'S LOVE WILL KEEP YOU SAFE

Prov 4:23-26

23 Keep thy heart with all diligence; for out of it are the issues of life. **24** Put away from thee a froward mouth, and perverse lips put far from thee. **25** Let thine eyes look right on, and let thine eyelids look straight before thee. **26** Ponder the path of thy feet, and let all thy ways be established. KJV

In love God puts His arms around you to keep you safe. His love will keep you safe, if you will allow Him in your life, His part is to love us, our part is to let Him do it. He tells us in these scriptures how to do our part, He already knows how to do his.

LET HIM IN AND HAVE A GREAT DAY.

"IN GOD WE TRUST"

Pastor Ray

SEPTEMBER 5

PUT YOUR TRUST IN GOD AND REJOICE

Ps 5:11-12

11 But let all those that put their trust in thee rejoice: let them ever shout for joy, because thou defendest them: let them also that love thy name be joyful in thee. **12** For thou, Lord, wilt bless the righteous; with favour wilt thou compass him as with a shield. KJV

God will never turn you away, you may not like what He offers, but it is you that is turning it down, not God refusing to give it to you.

RUN INTO HIS OPEN ARMS, AND BE BLESSED.

"IN GOD WE TRUST"

Pastor Ray

SEPTEMBER 6

LET GOD SET YOU FREE

Prov 6:1-5

My son, if thou be surety for thy friend, if thou hast stricken thy hand with a stranger, **2** Thou art snared with the words of thy mouth, thou art taken with the words of thy mouth. **3** Do this now, my son, deliver thyself, when thou art come into the hand of thy friend; go, humble thyself, and make sure thy friend. **4** Give not sleep to thine eyes, nor slumber to thine eyelids. **5** Deliver thyself as a roe from the hand of the hunter, and as a bird from the hand of the fowler. KJV

God is telling us to be careful who we chose as friends, and who we listen to, don't let yourself get drawn into something you can't get out of, pray over every deal before you make it.

PRAY, STUDY GOD'S WORD AND BE FREE. HAVE A GREAT DAY

"IN GOD WE TRUST"

Pastor Ray

SEPTEMBER 7

FEAR NOT

Rev 1:17-18

17 And when I saw him, I fell at his feet as dead. And he laid his right hand upon me, saying unto me, Fear not; I am the first and the last: **18** I am he that liveth, and was dead; and, behold, I am alive for evermore, Amen; and have the keys of hell and of death. KJV

Rev 1:17-18

17 When I saw Him, I fell at His feet as if dead. But He laid His right hand on me and said, Do not be afraid! I am the First and the Last, **18** And the Ever-living One [I am living in the eternity of the eternities]. I died, but see, I am alive forevermore; and I possess the keys of death and Hades (the realm of the dead). AMP

Fear not, is what God would say to you, for He knows that fear activates the devil and that faith will activates Himself. He knows that He has not given us a spirit of fear. A saying to remember. Fear knocked at the door, faith answered and there was no one there. Open your faith door, it keeps the devil out, and lets God in.

FEAR NOT, WALK WITH GOD, AND HAVE A GREAT DAY.

"IN GOD WE TRUST"

SEPTEMBER 8

ARE YOU LOOKING FOR A BETTER LIFE?

Prov 8:32-36

32 Now therefore hearken unto me, O ye children: for blessed are they that keep my ways. **33** Hear instruction, and be wise, and refuse it not. **34** Blessed is the man that heareth me, watching daily at my gates, waiting at the posts of my doors. **35** For whoso findeth me findeth life, and shall obtain favour of the Lord. **36** But he that sinneth against me wrongeth his own soul: all they that hate me love death. KJV

Seek wisdom daily, when you find her early each day, you will then have Gods knowledge on how to successfully get through each day with God as your partner and guide, avoiding the pitfalls your enemy sets before you, walking hand in hand with God the Father, God the Son, and God the Holy Spirit, being guided and protected every step of the way as you enjoy your better life.

HOLD TIGHTLY TO THEIR HANDS, AND HAVE A GREAT DAY

"IN GOD WE TRUST"

Pastor Ray

SEPTEMBER 9

YOU ARE CARED FOR

John 14:18-21

18 I will not leave you comfortless: I will come to you. **19** Yet a little while, and the world seeth me no more; but ye see me: because I live, ye shall live also. **20** At that day ye shall know that I am in my Father, and ye in me, and I in you. **21** He that hath my commandments, and keepeth them, he it is that loveth me: and he that loveth me shall be loved of my Father, and I will love him, and will manifest myself to him. KJV

God cares for you and doe's not want you to ever be alone, He will send the Holy Spirit to comfort you, teach you, and bring to your remembrance every thing that He has said to you. When you made Jesus lord of your life, He came in with God The Father in Him, with the promise that He would let you see Him and spiritually make Himself known to you. Don't shut Him out, read your bible so that the Holy Spirit will have something to bring to your remembrance.

RECEIVE AND BE BLESSED, HAVE A GREAT AND PROSPEROUS DAY

"IN GOD WE TRUST"

Pastor Ray

SEPTEMBER 10

THE BATTLE IS GOD'S

2 Chronicles 20:15

15 And he said, Hearken ye, all Judah, and ye inhabitants of Jerusalem, and thou king Jehoshaphat, Thus saith the LORD unto you, Be not afraid nor dismayed by reason of this great multitude; for the battle is not yours, but God's. KJV

Don't be afraid, God is on your side, and He has enough warriors to fight any battle and win. Our problem is having enough faith to let Him do it rather than trying to take care of the problem ourselves. But remember that this promise of God is for you today. You could read it this way "Hearken, all you inhabitants of the world" be not afraid, the battle is God's, not yours.

LET GO AND LET GOD! HAVE A GREAT DAY.

"IN GOD WE TRUST"

Pastor Ray

SEPTEMBER 11

GOD WANTS YOU TO HAVE A GOOD LIFE

Prov 11:30-31

30 The fruit of the righteous is a tree of life; and he that winneth souls is wise. **31** Behold, the righteous shall be recompensed in the earth: much more the wicked and the sinner. KJV

If we stay in right standing with the Lord, then we can expect a good and prosperous life. The devil will try his best to steal it from you just like he did with Adam and Eve, but we have been given the power to submit ourselves to God and resist the devil and all of his schemes to trick us into sin. Don't let yourself get into the position of finding what is in store for the bad.

LET GOD IN AND KEEP THE DEVIL OUT. HAVE A GREAT AND ENJOYABLE DAY

"IN GOD WE TRUST"

SEPTEMBER 12

DON'T BE AFRAID TO SPEAK TO YOUR MOUNTAIN

Mark 11:22-26

22 And Jesus answering saith unto them, Have faith in God.23 For verily I say unto you, That whosoever shall say unto this mountain, Be thou removed, and be thou cast into the sea; and shall not doubt in his heart, but shall believe that those things which he saith shall come to pass; he shall have whatsoever he saith. 24 Therefore I say unto you, What things soever ye desire, when ye pray, believe that ye receive them, and ye shall have them. 25 And when ye stand praying, forgive, if ye have ought against any: that your Father also which is in heaven may forgive you your trespasses. 26 But if ye do not forgive, neither will your Father which is in heaven forgive your trespasses. KJV

What is your mountain? Debt, loneliness, grief, sickness, relationships, whatever it is speak to it in Jesus name, believe with all your heart in Gods ability to remove the mountain. Then you can prayerfully thank Him for it until you see the manifestation of its removal. If we will do our part, God will do His.

FORGIVE, LET GO AND LET GOD. HAVE A GREAT DAY.

"IN GOD WE TRUST"

September 13

PAY ATTENTION AND LIVE

Prov 13:12-15

12 Hope deferred maketh the heart sick: but when the desire cometh, it is a tree of life. **13** Whoso despiseth the word shall be destroyed: but he that feareth the commandment shall be rewarded. **14** The law of the wise is a fountain of life, to depart from the snares of death. **15** Good understanding giveth favour: but the way of transgressors is hard. KJV

BELIEVE AND RECEIVE. LET GOD GRANT YOU A BEAUTIFUL PROSPEROUS AND HAPPY DAY

"IN GOD WE TRUST"

SEPTEMBER 14

YOU ARE PROVIDED AN ESCAPE ROUTE TO SAFETY

Prov 14:26-27

26 In the fear of the Lord is strong confidence: and his children shall have a place of refuge. **27** The fear of the Lord is a fountain of life, to depart from the snares of death. KJV

Prov 14:26-27

26 In the reverent and worshipful fear of the Lord there is strong confidence, and His children shall always have a place of refuge. 27 Reverent and worshipful fear of the Lord is a fountain of life, that one may avoid the snares of death. AMP

The fear (reverence) of God builds strong confidence in Him, every time we receive the victory in a situation our confidence in His ability to stand behind His word grows, until we become strong in faith, and when we are secure, and know our children are safe, we can walk boldly through our sojourn here on earth with no concern about what we should drink or eat. There are very few wells left to drink from, and we won't drink from a bad one. If you are buying bottled goods you won't buy one marked poison, you will pick the one with fresh clean water. Walk hand in hand with God, let Him take you down the path of righteousness to victory.

HAVE A GREAT, HAPPY AND PROSPEROUS DAY

"IN GOD WE TRUST"

SEPTEMBER 15

GOD'S LOVE IS NEVER CHANGING

Ps 15:1-3

Lord, who shall abide in thy tabernacle? who shall dwell in thy holy hill? **2** He that walketh uprightly, and worketh righteousness, and speaketh the truth in his heart. **3** He that backbiteth not with his tongue, nor doeth evil to his neighbour, nor taketh up a reproach against his neighbour. KJV

Ps 15:1-3

1 LORD, WHO shall dwell [temporarily] in Your tabernacle? Who shall dwell [permanently] on Your holy hill? 2 He who walks and lives uprightly and blamelessly, who works rightness and justice and speaks and thinks the truth in his heart, 3 He who does not slander with his tongue, nor does evil to his friend, nor takes up a reproach against his neighbor; AMP

God's invitation to come and dine, and live with Him, is always open to us, and when we get there He greets us with open arms, and when we step through His door we come into His presence in total health, dressed in the finest attire ready to enjoy our meal and His company forever. He stands at our door and knocks until we open the door and invite Him in.

OPEN YOUR DOOR, INVITE HIM IN, AND HAVE A GREAT DAY

"IN GOD WE TRUST"

Pastor Ray

SEPTEMBER 16

DO NOT FEAR

Isa 41:10-13

10 Fear thou not; for I am with thee: be not dismayed; for I am thy God: I will strengthen thee; yea, I will help thee; yea, I will uphold thee with the right hand of my righteousness. **11** Behold, all they that were incensed against thee shall be ashamed and confounded: they shall be as nothing; and they that strive with thee shall perish. **12** Thou shalt seek them, and shalt not find them, even them that contended with thee: they that war against thee shall be as nothing, and as a thing of nought. **13** For I the Lord thy God will hold thy right hand, saying unto thee, Fear not; I will help thee. KJV

Isa 41:10-13

10 Fear not [there is nothing to fear], for I am with you; do not look around you in terror and be dismayed, for I am your God. I will strengthen and harden you to difficulties, yes, I will help you; yes, I will hold you up and retain you with My [victorious] right hand of rightness and justice. 11 Behold, all they who are enraged and inflamed against you shall be put to shame and confounded; they who strive against you shall be as nothing and shall perish. 12 You shall seek those who contend with you but shall not find them; they who war against you shall be as nothing, as nothing at all. 13 For I the Lord your God hold your right hand; I am the Lord, Who says to you, Fear not; I will help you! AMP

God is faithful to keep His word, what He has promised, that He will do, so stay strong, don't be afraid to do what you know is right. What God calls you to do will come to pass, if you will yield to Him and be obedient, He will see you through to victory, every time.

HAVE FAITH IN GOD. HAVE A GREAT DAY.

"IN GOD WE TRUST"

Pastor Ray

SEPTEMBER 17

PURE LOVE

Phil 1:15-18

15 Some indeed preach Christ even of envy and strife; and some also of good will: **16** The one preach Christ of contention, not sincerely, supposing to add affliction to my bonds: **17** But the other of love, knowing that I am set for the defence of the gospel. **18** What then? notwithstanding, every way, whether in pretence, or in truth, Christ is preached; and I therein do rejoice, yea, and will rejoice. KJV

Phil 1:15-18

15 Some, it is true, [actually] preach Christ (the Messiah) [for no better reason than] out of envy and rivalry (party spirit), but others are doing so out of a loyal spirit and goodwill. 16 The latter [proclaim Christ] out of love, because they recognize and know that I am [providentially] put here for the defense of the good news (the Gospel). 17 But the former preach Christ out of a party spirit, insincerely [out of no pure motive, but thinking to annoy me], supposing they are making my bondage more bitter and my chains more galling. 18 But what does it matter, so long as either way, whether in pretense [for personal ends] or in all honesty [for the furtherance of the Truth], Christ is being proclaimed? And in that I [now] rejoice, yes, and I shall rejoice [hereafter] also. AMP

God's love for you is as pure as highly refined gold, given to you freely, His blessings are beyond numbering, and He wants you to have them all, But how do you receive them? as pure love without strings attached, or as a debt paid. God doe's not owe us anything, so let us open our hearts to give and receive love as just pure love with nothing tied to it. God want us to love Him just like He loves us.

LET YOUR LOVE FLOW AND ENJOY THE RETURN. HAVE A GREAT DAY.

"IN GOD WE TRUST"

SEPTEMBER 18

YOU CAN'T FOOL GOD

Gal 6:7-8

7 Be not deceived; God is not mocked: for whatsoever a man soweth, that shall he also reap. **8** For he that soweth to his flesh shall of the flesh reap corruption; but he that soweth to the Spirit shall of the Spirit reap life everlasting. KJV

Gal 6:7-8

7 Do not be deceived *and* deluded *and* misled; God will not allow Himself to be sneered at (scorned, disdained, or mocked by mere pretensions or professions, or by His precepts being set aside.) [He inevitably deludes himself who attempts to delude God.] For whatever a man sows, that *and* that only is what he will reap. **8** For he who sows to his own flesh (lower nature, sensuality) will from the flesh reap decay *and* ruin *and* destruction, but he who sows to the Spirit will from the Spirit reap eternal life. AMP

Do you want a good life worth living? Then start planting or sowing what you would like to receive, if you want love then sow it, if you want friends then sow friendship, if you want people to speak good things about you, then say good thing about others, what you say is what you get.

CONTROL YOUR TONGUE. HAVE A BEAUTIFUL, HAPPY, AND PROSPEROUS DAY.

"IN GOD WE TRUST"

SEPTEMBER 19

YOU ARE NOT FORGOTTEN

Ps 9:17-20

17 The wicked shall be turned into hell, and all the nations that forget God. **18** For the needy shall not alway be forgotten: the expectation of the poor shall not perish for ever. **19** Arise, O Lord; let not man prevail: let the heathen be judged in thy sight. **20** Put them in fear, O Lord: that the nations may know themselves to be but men. Selah. KJV

Be sincere with God, for He knows when we are trying to con Him into doing something for us that we really don't need, God tells us in second Chronicles;7:14 that if we His people will humble ourselves, pray, seek His face, and turn from our wicked ways; then will I hear from heaven, and will forgive our sin, and will heal our land. Our part is to submit to Him and let Him take care of it.

BE OBEDIENT, PRAY AND LET GOD HANDLE IT, HAVE A NICE DAY.

"IN GOD WE TRUST

Pastor Ray

SEPTEMBER 20

WHO CAN BE AGAINST YOU

Deut 11:25-28

25 There shall no man be able to stand before you: for the Lord your God shall lay the fear of you and the dread of you upon all the land that ye shall tread upon, as he hath said unto you. **26** Behold, I set before you this day a blessing and a curse; **27** A blessing, if ye obey the commandments of the Lord your God, which I command you this day: **28** And a curse, if ye will not obey the commandments of the Lord your God, but turn aside out of the way which I command you this day, to go after other gods, which ye have not known. KJV

God will go before you to prepare the way for you to be successful, wherever He sends you or whatever He calls you to do, He will make the way and give you the provisions needed to win, in other words He (God) is all you need, you and He are the majority.

BE BLESSED AND HAVE A GREAT DAY

"IN GOD WE TRUST"

Pastor Ray

SEPTEMBER 21

DON'T CONDEMN YOURSELF

Rom 8:1-3

8 There is therefore now no condemnation to them which are in Christ Jesus, who walk not after the flesh, but after the Spirit. 2 For the law of the Spirit of life in Christ Jesus hath made me free from the law of sin and death. 3 For what the law could not do, in that it was weak through the flesh, God sending his own Son in the likeness of sinful flesh, and for sin, condemned sin in the flesh: KJV

We are our own worst enemies when it comes to condemnation, some of us are struggling with self forgiveness, as we can easily remember the things we have done. Yet when we run to God asking forgiveness, (instead of from Him, condemning ourselves) He is quick to forgive and forget our sins. How can He condemn us for something He refuses to remember? You are loved and forgiven the moment you ask Him to forgive you for what you have done and He never condemns you for it.

LET GOD BE YOUR FRIEND, HAVE A NICE DAY

"IN GOD WE TRUST"

Pastor Ray

SEPTEMBER 22

GOD CARES FOR YOU

1 Peter 5:5-7

5 Likewise, ye younger, submit yourselves unto the elder. Yea, all of you be subject one to another, and be clothed with humility: for God resisteth the proud, and giveth grace to the humble. **6** Humble yourselves therefore under the mighty hand of God, that he may exalt you in due time: **7** Casting all your care upon him; for he careth for you. KJV

Gods love for you is never ending, He loves and cares for you during the good and the bad. It doe's not matter to Him how rotten we have been, God is always looking for some one to receive His love, and love Him in return, so let us humble ourselves, love each other, and walk hand in hand with God, rolling all of our cares over on Him.

HAVE A BEAUTIFUL AND HAPPY DAY.

"IN GOD WE TRUST"

Pastor Ray

SEPTEMBER 23

GOD'S WORD FOR YOU

3 John 1

2 Beloved, I pray that you may prosper in every way and [that your body] may keep well, even as [I know] your soul keeps well and prospers. AMP

God wants you healthy, prosperous, and wise in every area of your life, give in to Him, let Him lead you to your expected destination.

HAVE A BEAUTIFUL AND HAPPY DAY.

"IN GOD WE TRUST"

SEPTEMBER 24

WHERE THERE IS A WILL, THERE IS A WAY

Luke 6:36-38

36 Be ye therefore merciful, as your Father also is merciful. **37** Judge not, and ye shall not be judged: condemn not, and ye shall not be condemned: forgive, and ye shall be forgiven: **38** Give, and it shall be given unto you; good measure, pressed down, and shaken together, and running over, shall men give into your bosom. For with the same measure that ye mete withal it shall be measured to you again. KJV

God always provides a way for us to receive His blessings, how?, by giving what you want to receive, study these scriptures and then apply them to your life and see what happens.

YOU WILL BE BLESSED. HAVE A GREAT DAY.

"IN GOD WE TRUST"

Pastor Ray

SEPTEMBER 25

HOW TO GET YOUR NEED MET

Matt 6:31-33

31 Therefore take no thought, saying, What shall we eat? or, What shall we drink? or, Wherewithal shall we be clothed? **32** (For after all these things do the Gentiles seek:) for your heavenly Father knoweth that ye have need of all these things. **33** But seek ye first the kingdom of God, and his righteousness; and all these things shall be added unto you. KJV

Our part is to diligently seek God's kingdom and His righteousness, and not be concerned with what we shall wear today, or what we shall have for dinner? He knows our every need, and will make known to you the answers as we need them, for example, when your waitress comes to the table, the first thing she/he asks is, what will you have to drink? and God quickly gives you the answer.

CONCENTRATE ON THE KINGDOM, NOT THE NEED.

"IN GOD WE TRUST"

Pastor Ray

SEPTEMBER 26

YOU HAVE OVERCOME

1 John 4:2-4

2 Hereby know ye the Spirit of God: Every spirit that confesseth that Jesus Christ is come in the flesh is of God: **3** And every spirit that confesseth not that Jesus Christ is come in the flesh is not of God: and this is that spirit of antichrist, whereof ye have heard that it should come; and even now already is it in the world. **4** Ye are of God, little children, and have overcome them: because greater is he that is in you, than he that is in the world. KJV

When we accepted Jesus as Lord of our lives, He (the greater one) came to reside in us, and has given us the victory over the demonic spirits of the world. Notice that the AMP says you have already won a victory, because Jesus that resides in us is far greater than any thing in the world. (Have already) is past tense, so let us not cower, but walk and live in the victory Jesus has given us.

BE STRONG IN THE LORD, STAND YOUR GROUND, FOR IN HIM WE ARE VICTORIOUS. HAVE A GREAT DAY.

"IN GOD WE TRUST"

Pastor Ray

SEPTEMBER 27

DON'T BE AFRAID

Ps 27:1-3

The Lord is my light and my salvation; whom shall I fear? the Lord is the strength of my life; of whom shall I be afraid? **2** When the wicked, even mine enemies and my foes, came upon me to eat up my flesh, they stumbled and fell. **3** Though an host should encamp against me, my heart shall not fear: though war should rise against me, in this will I be confident. We are told in Ps 27:14 to Wait on the Lord: be of good courage, and he shall strengthen thine heart: wait, I say, on the Lord. KJV

Fear not, God is with you, He shall protect you and keep you safe, as long as you stay with Him. He is on your side, don't let the ways of the world draw you away from your source of security.

STAY WITH GOD, STAY COOL, AND HAVE A GREAT DAY.

"IN GOD WE TRUST"

Pastor Ray

SEPTEMBER 28

REMEMBER, GOD IS STILL ON YOUR SIDE

Ps 28:6-7

6 Blessed be the Lord, because he hath heard the voice of my supplications. **7** The Lord is my strength and my shield; my heart trusted in him, and I am helped: therefore my heart greatly rejoiceth; and with my song will I praise him. KJV

God never changes, once we have accepted Jesus as Lord of our lives, God has promised never to leave us or forsake us, He is always with us and on our side, to help us win our battles, with all temptations, sickness and etc. His Word says in 1 Peter 2:24 Who his own self bare our sins in his own body on the tree, that we, being dead to sins, should live unto righteousness: by whose stripes ye were healed. Were is past tenses, so let us walk in the health that God has already provided.

BE BLESSED, AND HAVE A GREAT DAY.

"IN GOD WE TRUST"

Pastor Ray

SEPTEMBER 29

YOUR TRUST IN THE LORD BRINGS YOU TO A SAFE PLACE

Prov 29:15, 17, 25

15 The rod and reproof give wisdom: but a child left to himself bringeth his mother to shame. **17** Correct thy son, and he shall give thee rest; yea, he shall give delight unto thy soul. **25** The fear of man bringeth a snare: but whoso putteth his trust in the Lord shall be safe. KJV

God is telling us here, how to have a happy home, and not be concerned about what others think of us, having no fear of mankind, and putting our trust in God to live in a safe place under His guidance and protection.

HAVE A GREAT AND BEAUTIFUL DAY,

"IN GOD WE TRUST"

SEPTEMBER 30

IF YOU CAN'T SAY SOMETHING GOOD DON'T SPEAK,

Prov 30:32-33

32 If thou hast done foolishly in lifting up thyself, or if thou hast thought evil, lay thine hand upon thy mouth. 33 Surely the churning of milk bringeth forth butter, and the wringing of the nose bringeth forth blood: so the forcing of wrath bringeth forth strife. KJV

God has given us the ability to think and speak, not the ability to speak and then think about what we have said, so let us put our brains in gear before we open our mouths to speak. Words can be very hurtful, think and then speak words that will bless the hearer, and not give them a bloody nose. I have heard many people say I wish I hadn't said that, and some of them had just stepped out of the pulpit at church.

LET YOUR WORDS BE A BLESSING, HAVE A GREAT DAY

"IN GOD WE TRUST"

Pastor Ray

OCTOBER 1

GOD LIKES YOU

Ps 1:1-3

1 Blessed is the man that walketh not in the counsel of the ungodly, nor standeth in the way of sinners, nor sitteth in the seat of the scornful. **2** But his delight is in the law of the Lord; and in his law doth he meditate day and night. **3** And he shall be like a tree planted by the rivers of water, that bringeth forth his fruit in his season; his leaf also shall not wither; and whatsoever he doeth shall prosper. KJV

Ps 1:1-3

1 BLESSED (HAPPY, fortunate, prosperous, and enviable) is the man who walks and lives not in the counsel of the ungodly [following their advice, their plans and purposes], nor stands [submissive and inactive] in the path where sinners walk, nor sits down [to relax and rest] where the scornful [and the mockers] gather. 2 But his delight and desire are in the law of the Lord, and on His law (the precepts, the instructions, the teachings of God) he habitually meditates (ponders and studies) by day and by night. 3 And he shall be like a tree firmly planted [and tended] by the streams of water, ready to bring forth its fruit in its season; its leaf also shall not fade or wither; and everything he does shall prosper [and come to maturity]. AMP

God not only likes you, he loves you as well, and has made provisions for you to be successful, but it is up to you to accept those provisions and act on them. (Jer 29:11 For I know the plans I have for you," declares the Lord, "plans to prosper you and not to harm you, plans to give you hope and a future. NIV)

STUDY HIS WORD, WALK TALL AND TRUE BEFORE GOD AND MAN, AND BE BLESSED. HAVE A WONDERFUL DAY.

"IN GOD WE TRUST"

OCTOBER 2

YOUR REVERENCE OF GOD BRINGS KNOWLEDGE

Prov 2:1-5

2 My son, if thou wilt receive my words, and hide my commandments with thee; **2** So that thou incline thine ear unto wisdom, and apply thine heart to understanding; **3** Yea, if thou criest after knowledge, and liftest up thy voice for understanding; **4** If thou seekest her as silver, and searchest for her as for hid treasures; **5** Then shalt thou understand the fear of the Lord, and find the knowledge of God. KJV

Prov 2:1-5

1 MY SON, if you will receive my words and treasure up my commandments within you, 2 Making your ear attentive to skillful and godly Wisdom and inclining and directing your heart and mind to understanding [applying all your powers to the quest for it]; 3 Yes, if you cry out for insight and raise your voice for understanding, 4 If you seek [Wisdom] as for silver and search for skillful and godly Wisdom as for hidden treasures, 5 Then you will understand the reverent and worshipful fear of the Lord and find the knowledge of [our omniscient] God. AMP

Be persistent in your pursuit of a relationship with Jesus. Open your heart and let Him come in and show you the perfect way into His wisdom and knowledge.

SEEK FIRST THE KINGDOM GOD AND HIS RIGHTEOUSNESS, AND HAVE A VERY GOOD DAY

"IN GOD WE TRUST"

OCTOBER 3

HAVING TROUBLE SLEEPING?, DON'T BE AFRAID

Prov 3:21-26

21 My son, let not them depart from thine eyes: keep sound wisdom and discretion: 22 So shall they be life unto thy soul, and grace to thy neck. 23 Then shalt thou walk in thy way safely, and thy foot shall not stumble. 24 When thou liest down, thou shalt not be afraid: yea, thou shalt lie down, and thy sleep shall be sweet. 25 Be not afraid of sudden fear, neither of the desolation of the wicked, when it cometh. 26 For the Lord shall be thy confidence, and shall keep thy foot from being taken. KJV

Prov 3:21-26

21 My son, let them not escape from your sight, but keep sound and godly Wisdom and discretion, 22 And they will be life to your inner self, and a gracious ornament to your neck (your outer self). 23 Then you will walk in your way securely and in confident trust, and you shall not dash your foot or stumble. 24 When you lie down, you shall not be afraid; yes, you shall lie down, and your sleep shall be sweet. 25 Be not afraid of sudden terror and panic, nor of the stormy blast or the storm and ruin of the wicked when it comes [for you will be guiltless], 26 For the Lord shall be your confidence, firm and strong, and shall keep your foot from being caught [in a trap or some hidden danger]. AMP

This is God's promise for you, so have no fear of not waking up, enjoy your nap, have a good nights sleep, looking forward to what God has in store for you, for He is going to keep you safe and secure, as long as we allow Him to lead. We can pull away from Him any time and stop the blessing, the choice is ours,

REJOICE: YOUR WAY IS SECURE, DON'T LET WORRY STEAL YOUR JOY OR SLEEP. HAVE A GREAT DAY.

"IN GOD WE TRUST"

OCTOBER 4

GOD'S LOVE WILL KEEP YOU SAFE

Prov 4:23-27

23 Keep thy heart with all diligence; for out of it are the issues of life. 24 Put away from thee a froward mouth, and perverse lips put far from thee. 25 Let thine eyes look right on, and let thine eyelids look straight before thee. 26 Ponder the path of thy feet, and let all thy ways be established. 27 Turn not to the right hand nor to the left: remove thy foot from evil. KJV

Prov 4:23-27

23 Keep and guard your heart with all vigilance and above all that you guard, for out of it flow the springs of life. 24 Put away from you false and dishonest speech, and willful and contrary talk put far from you. 25 Let your eyes look right on [with fixed purpose], and let your gaze be straight before you. 26 Consider well the path of your feet, and let all your ways be established and ordered aright. 27 Turn not aside to the right hand or to the left; remove your foot from evil. AMP

In love God puts His arms around you to keep you safe. His love will keep you safe, if you will allow him in your life, His part is to love us, our part is to let Him do it. He tells us in these scriptures how to do our part, He already knows how to do his.

LET HIM IN, AND HAVE A SAFE, PROSPEROUS, HAPPY DAY.

"IN GOD WE TRUST"

OCTOBER 5

PUT YOUR TRUST IN GOD AND REJOICE

Ps 5:11-12

11 But let all those that put their trust in thee rejoice: let them ever shout for joy, because thou defendest them: let them also that love thy name be joyful in thee. **12** For thou, Lord, wilt bless the righteous; with favour wilt thou compass him as with a shield. KJV

Ps 5:11-12

11 But let all those who take refuge and put their trust in You rejoice; let them ever sing and shout for joy, because You make a covering over them and defend them; let those also who love Your name be joyful in You and be in high spirits. 12 For You, Lord, will bless the [uncompromisingly] righteous [him who is upright and in right standing with You]; as with a shield You will surround him with goodwill (pleasure and favor). AMP

God will never turn you away, you may not like what he offers, but it is you that is turning it down, not God refusing to give it to you.

RUN INTO HIS OPEN ARMS, AND BE BLESSED. HAVE A GREAT DAY.

"IN GOD WE TRUST"

Pastor Ray

OCTOBER 6

LET GOD SET YOU FREE

Prov 6:1-5

My son, if thou be surety for thy friend, if thou hast stricken thy hand with a stranger, **2** Thou art snared with the words of thy mouth, thou art taken with the words of thy mouth. **3** Do this now, my son, deliver thyself, when thou art come into the hand of thy friend; go, humble thyself, and make sure thy friend. **4** Give not sleep to thine eyes, nor slumber to thine eyelids. **5** Deliver thyself as a roe from the hand of the hunter, and as a bird from the hand of the fowler. KJV

Prov 6:1-5

6 1 My child, if you have put up security for a friend's debt or agreed to guarantee the debt of a stranger—2 if you have trapped yourself by your agreement and are caught by what you said—3 follow my advice and save yourself, for you have placed yourself at your friend's mercy. Now swallow your pride; go and beg to have your name erased. 4 Don't put it off; do it now! Don't rest until you do. 5 Save yourself like a gazelle escaping from a hunter, like a bird fleeing from a net.

God is telling us to be careful who we chose as friends, and who we listen to, don't let yourself get drawn into something you can't get out of, pray over every deal before you make it.

PRAY, STUDY GOD'S WORD AND BE FREE. HAVE A GREAT DAY

"IN GOD WE TRUST"

OCTOBER 7

GOD'S LOVE FOR YOU IS NEVER ENDING

Ps 7:8-9

8 The Lord shall judge the people: judge me, O Lord, according to my righteousness, and according to mine integrity that is in me. **9** Oh let the wickedness of the wicked come to an end; but establish the just: for the righteous God trieth the hearts and reins. KJV

Ps 7:8-9

8 The Lord judges the people; judge me, O Lord, and do me justice according to my righteousness [my rightness, justice, and right standing with You] and according to the integrity that is in me. 9 Oh, let the wickedness of the wicked come to an end, but establish the [uncompromisingly] righteous [those upright and in harmony with You]; for You, Who try the hearts and emotions and thinking powers, are a righteous God. AMP

God works with us, He shapes and molds us into what he wants us to be, then He cleans and polishes us to perfection, a fit vessel to live with Him for eternity. How long this will take depends on our willingness to yield to His correction. He will never give up on us, but we can give up on ourselves.

DON'T GIVE UP, YIELD TO HIS LOVE, AND ENJOY YOUR DAY.

"IN GOD WE TRUST"

Pastor Ray

OCTOBER 8

ARE YOU LOOKING FOR A BETTER LIFE?

Prov 8:32-36

32 Now therefore hearken unto me, O ye children: for blessed are they that keep my ways. **33** Hear instruction, and be wise, and refuse it not. **34** Blessed is the man that heareth me, watching daily at my gates, waiting at the posts of my doors. **35** For whoso findeth me findeth life, and shall obtain favour of the Lord. **36** But he that sinneth against me wrongeth his own soul: all they that hate me love death. KJV

Prov 8:32-36

32 Now therefore listen to me, O you sons; for blessed (happy, fortunate, to be envied) are those who keep my ways. 33 Hear instruction and be wise, and do not refuse or neglect it. 34 Blessed (happy, fortunate, to be envied) is the man who listens to me, watching daily at my gates, waiting at the posts of my doors. 35 For whoever finds me [Wisdom] finds life and draws forth and obtains favor from the Lord. 36 But he who misses me or sins against me wrongs and injures himself; all who hate me love and court death. AMP

Seek wisdom daily, when you find her early each day, you will then have Gods knowledge on how to successfully get through each day with God as your partner and guide, avoiding the pitfalls your enemy sets before you, walking hand in hand with God the Father, God the Son, and God the Holy Spirit, being guided and protected every step of the way as you enjoy your better life.

HOLD TIGHTLY TO THEIR HANDS, AND HAVE A GREAT DAY

"IN GOD WE TRUST"

OCTOBER 9

SEEK WISDOM, AND LIVE LONG AND WELL

Prov 9:9-12

9 Give instruction to a wise man, and he will be yet wiser: teach a just man, and he will increase in learning. **10** The fear of the Lord is the beginning of wisdom: and the knowledge of the holy is understanding. **11** For by me thy days shall be multiplied, and the years of thy life shall be increased. **12** If thou be wise, thou shalt be wise for thyself: but if thou scornest, thou alone shalt bear it. KJV

Prov 9:9-12

9 Give instruction to a wise man and he will be yet wiser; teach a righteous man (one upright and in right standing with God) and he will increase in learning. 10 The reverent and worshipful fear of the Lord is the beginning (the chief and choice part) of Wisdom, and the knowledge of the Holy One is insight and understanding. 11 For by me [Wisdom from God] your days shall be multiplied, and the years of your life shall be increased. 12 If you are wise, you are wise for yourself; if you scorn, you alone will bear it and pay the penalty. AMP

These scriptures tell us to diligently seek God and we shall find Him, (Jer 29:13 And ye shall seek me, and find me, when ye shall search for me with all your heart.) When we receive Jesus as the Lord of our lives, that is the beginning of our training for God's wisdom and knowledge, and when we have finished our training we will be sent forth to share what we have learned with others. Study the bible to show your self approved.

BE BLESSED, AND HAVE A GREAT AND HAPPY DAY.

"IN GOD WE TRUST"

Pastor Ray

OCTOBER 10

GODS LOVE FOR YOU CONTINUES FOREVER

Psalm 100:3-5

3 Know ye that the LORD he is God: it is he that hath made us, and not we ourselves; we are his people, and the sheep of his pasture. 4 Enter into his gates with thanksgiving, and into his courts with praise: be thankful unto him, and bless his name. 5 For the LORD is good; his mercy is everlasting; and his truth endureth to all generations. KJV

Ps 100:3-5

3 Know (perceive, recognize, and understand with approval) that the Lord is God! It is He Who has made us, not we ourselves [and we are His]! We are His people and the sheep of His pasture. 4 Enter into His gates with thanksgiving and a thank offering and into His courts with praise! Be thankful and say so to Him, bless and affectionately praise His name! 5 For the Lord is good; His mercy and loving-kindness are everlasting, His faithfulness and truth endure to all generations. AMP

We are told in the scriptures that Jesus, the Word, made all things, (John 1:1-3 In the beginning was the Word, and the Word was with God, and the Word was God. 2 The same was in the beginning with God. 3 All things were made by him; and without him was not any thing made that was made. KJV) That includes you and I, and I am very thankful that God's mercy endures forever. He waited for me to wake up and know who He is. And now I am thankful for the peace that He gives me in all situations.

RECEIVE HIS PEACE, LET YOUR HEART REJOICE, AND HAVE A GREAT DAY.

"IN GOD WE TRUST"

OCTOBER 11

GOD SEES YOU THE WAY YOU WILL BE

2 Cor 5:17-18

17 Therefore if any man be in Christ, he is a new creature: old things are passed away; behold, all things are become new. **18** And all things are of God, who hath reconciled us to himself by Jesus Christ, and hath given to us the ministry of reconciliation; KJV

2 Cor 5:17-18

17 Therefore if any person is [ingrafted] in Christ (the Messiah) he is a new creation (a new creature altogether); the old [previous moral and spiritual condition] has passed away. Behold, the fresh and new has come! 18 But all things are from God, Who through Jesus Christ reconciled us to Himself [received us into favor, brought us into harmony with Himself] and gave to us the ministry of reconciliation [that by word and deed we might aim to bring others into harmony with Him]. AMP

Did you ever hear the song, This old House? Or see someone buy an old house or an old car to fix up. That person doesn't see the house or the car as it is, but as it will be when he is finished with it, God is the same with us, He takes us just the way we are, then proceeds to change us into the finished product that only He can see, a beautiful creature created in His Image.

LET HIM CHANGE YOU, HAVE A BLESSED DAY

"IN GOD WE TRUST"

Pastor Ray

OCTOBER 12

GOD IS WITH YOU ALWAYS

Deut 4:29-31

29 But if from thence thou shalt seek the Lord thy God, thou shalt find him, if thou seek him with all thy heart and with all thy soul. **30** When thou art in tribulation, and all these things are come upon thee, even in the latter days, if thou turn to the Lord thy God, and shalt be obedient unto his voice; **31** (For the Lord thy God is a merciful God;) he will not forsake thee, neither destroy thee, nor forget the covenant of thy fathers which he sware unto them. KJV

Deut 4:29-31

29 But if from there you will seek (inquire for and require as necessity) the Lord your God, you will find Him if you [truly] seek Him with all your heart [and mind] and soul and life. 30 When you are in tribulation and all these things come upon you, in the latter days you will turn to the Lord your God and be obedient to His voice. 31 For the Lord your God is a merciful God; He will not fail you or destroy you or forget the covenant of your fathers, which He swore to them. AMP

When hard times come on you, run to God, don't run from Him. He promised long ago that He would be merciful if you would return to Him and that He would not forsake you. Know that He is with you always, even when you think He is not.

GOD WILL NEVER LET YOU GO, HANG ON, AND HAVE A GREAT DAY.

"IN GOD WE TRUST"

Pastor Ray

OCTOBER 13

SOUND THINKING LEADS TO LIFE

Prov 13:13-15

13 Whoso despiseth the word shall be destroyed: but he that feareth the commandment shall be rewarded. 14 The law of the wise is a fountain of life, to depart from the snares of death. 15 Good understanding giveth favour: but the way of transgressors is hard. KJV

Prov 13:13-15

13 Whoever despises the word and counsel [of God] brings destruction upon himself, but he who [reverently] fears and respects the commandment [of God] is rewarded. 14 The teaching of the wise is a fountain of life, that one may avoid the snares of death. 15 Good understanding wins favor, but the way of the transgressor is hard [like the barren, dry soil or the impassable swamp]. AMP

Why is it that the human race can not believe the word of our God and creator? Look at these scriptures (or instructions), The law or teaching of the wise is a fountain of life, if we seek it and find it, and then use it, we will wisely avoid the death traps. Good understanding will lead us to a favorable position with God, He tells us that the way of the transgressor is hard, but most of us will go our own way, get into trouble and then scream to God, How did you let this happen? God did not let it happen, we had to do it our way to prove that God knows what he is talking about,

THE WAY OF THE TRANSGRESSOR IS HARD,

STAY WITH GOD AND ENJOY YOUR DAY.

"IN GOD WE TRUST"

OCTOBER 14

YOU ARE NOT FORSAKEN

Heb 13:5-6

5 Let your conversation be without covetousness; and be content with such things as ye have: for he hath said, I will never leave thee, nor forsake thee.**6** So that we may boldly say, The Lord is my helper, and I will not fear what man shall do unto me. KJV

Heb 13:5-6

5 Let your character or moral disposition be free from love of money [including greed, avarice, lust, and craving for earthly possessions] and be satisfied with your present [circumstances and with what you have]; for He [God] Himself has said, I will not in any way fail you nor give you up nor leave you without support. [I will] not, [I will] not, [I will] not in any degree leave you helpless nor forsake nor let [you] down (relax My hold on you)! [Assuredly not!] 6 So we take comfort and are encouraged and confidently and boldly say, The Lord is my Helper; I will not be seized with alarm [I will not fear or dread or be terrified]. What can man do to me? AMP

This was a very encouraging scripture for me as I went through 24 days in the Hospital, eight years ago. There were times when I cried out to Him and it seemed that I was getting no answer, but He was right there all the time, I had to be still and know that he was God before I could hear Him. That is a hard thing to do when you have four different Doctors pushing pills and shots at you and telling you that's what it takes to get well, and you know that Jesus is your healer, but your the only one that believes that He is, while they are trying to convince you otherwise, but we won.

STAY WITH GOD, WALK IN VICTORY, AND HAVE A NICE DAY. HIS LOVE FOR YOU NEVER FAILS AND NEVER ENDS.

"IN GOD WE TRUST"

OCTOBER 15

YOU ARE GOD'S BELOVED

3 John 2

2 Beloved, I wish above all things that thou mayest prosper and be in health, even as thy soul prospereth. Col 1:12-13 Giving thanks unto the Father, which hath made us meet to be partakers of the inheritance of the saints in light:**13** Who hath delivered us from the power of darkness, and hath translated us into the kingdom of his dear Son: KJV

3 John 2

Beloved, I pray that you may prosper in every way and [that your body] may keep well, even as [I know] your soul keeps well and prospers. AMP

This is God's prayer for His children, those that believe in Him, have received Him and been translated into the kingdom of His dear Son. He wants you to be in good health and be prosperous in all that you do.

HAVE A PROSPEROUS AND HEALTHY DAY

"IN GOD WE TRUST"

Pastor Ray

OCTOBER 16

WITH GOD ON YOUR SIDE, YOU WIN

Rom 8:31-33

31 What shall we then say to these things? If God be for us, who can be against us? **32** He that spared not his own Son, but delivered him up for us all, how shall he not with him also freely give us all things? **33** Who shall lay any thing to the charge of God's elect? It is God that justifieth. KJV

Rom 8:31-33

31 What then shall we say to [all] this? If God is for us, who [can be] against us? [Who can be our foe, if God is on our side?] 32 He who did not withhold or spare [even] His own Son but gave Him up for us all, will He not also with Him freely and graciously give us all [other] things? 33 Who shall bring any charge against God's elect [when it is] God Who justifies [that is, Who puts us in right relation to Himself? Who shall come forward and accuse or impeach those whom God has chosen? Will God, Who acquits us?] AMP

When God is for us we have an army of His angels around us to see that we are protected. Our part is to rest assured that God means what He says, have faith in Him, and know that He is able to perform His Word. which is alive and life giving for all that receive it, and it is for Today.

KNOW THAT GOD IS WITH YOU ALL THE TIME, HAVE A GREAT DAY.

"IN GOD WE TRUST"

Pastor Ray

OCTOBER 17

YOU HAVE SOMEONE WHO CARES

1 Peter 5:7-9

7 Casting all your care upon him; for he careth for you. **8** Be sober, be vigilant; because your adversary the devil, as a roaring lion, walketh about, seeking whom he may devour: **9** Whom resist stedfast in the faith, knowing that the same afflictions are accomplished in your brethren that are in the world. KJV

1 Peter 5:7-9

7 Casting the whole of your care [all your anxieties, all your worries, all your concerns, once and for all] on Him, for He cares for you affectionately and cares about you watchfully. 8 Be well balanced (temperate, sober of mind), be vigilant and cautious at all times; for that enemy of yours, the devil, roams around like a lion roaring [in fierce hunger], seeking someone to seize upon and devour. 9 Withstand him; be firm in faith [against his onset—rooted, established, strong, immovable, and determined], knowing that the same (identical) sufferings are appointed to your brotherhood (the whole body of Christians) throughout the world. AMP

Let God help you through your trials and troubles, go to Him in prayer making your need known to Him, then leave them there with Him, for He loves you and cares for you and will see you through. He has seen me through many times in my 87 year sojourn on this earth and I know that what He has done for me He will do for YOU.

KEEP THE FAITH, STAY STRONG, AND HAVE A WONDERFUL DAY.

"IN GOD WE TRUST"

Pastor Ray

OCTOBER 18

IF YOU DON'T BELIEVE, YOU CANT RECEIVE

Matt 21:21-22

21 Jesus answered and said unto them, Verily I say unto you, If ye have faith, and doubt not, ye shall not only do this which is done to the fig tree, but also if ye shall say unto this mountain, Be thou removed, and be thou cast into the sea; it shall be done.22 And all things, whatsoever ye shall ask in prayer, believing, ye shall receive. KJV

Matt 21:21-22

21 And Jesus answered them, Truly I say to you, if you have faith (a firm relying trust) and do not doubt, you will not only do what has been done to the fig tree, but even if you say to this mountain, Be taken up and cast into the sea, it will be done. 22 And whatever you ask for in prayer, having faith and [really] believing, you will receive. AMP

When we ask God to help us in the name of Jesus, we can rest assured we will receive His help. When we pray according to His word, in faith believing without doubt, then we can expectantly wait for what we prayed for. There is more prayers going out to Him today than ever, let us all pray with faith in God that we are being led in the right direction so we can welcome Him back into our neighborhood, city, and nation.

HAVE FAITH IN GOD, BELIEVE AND RECEIVE. ENJOY YOUR DAY.

"IN GOD WE TRUST"

Pastor Ray

OCTOBER 19

WHAT YOU SAY IS WHAT YOU GET

Matt 15:17-20

17 Do not ye yet understand, that whatsoever entereth in at the mouth goeth into the belly, and is cast out into the draught? 18 But those things which proceed out of the mouth come forth from the heart; and they defile the man. 19 For out of the heart proceed evil thoughts, murders, adulteries, fornications, thefts, false witness, blasphemies: 20 These are the things which defile a man: but to eat with unwashen hands defileth not a man. KJV

Matt 15:17-20

17 Do you not see and understand that whatever goes into the mouth passes into the abdomen and so passes on into the place where discharges are deposited? 18 But whatever comes out of the mouth comes from the heart, and this is what makes a man unclean and defiles [him]. 19 For out of the heart come evil thoughts (reasonings and disputings and designs) such as murder, adultery, sexual vice, theft, false witnessing, slander, and irreverent speech. 20 These are what make a man unclean and defile [him]; but eating with unwashed hands does not make him unclean or defile [him]. AMP

If we cannot say something good we should not say anything, if we say the wrong thing it could destroy our relationships, our marriage, and even ourselves. If we keep saying we are no good, that's what we will be. If we keep running something down with our words, it will never get any better. What you say is what you get. Read the first chapter of Genesis and notice how many times God said and it was so. Let us take control of that deadly weapon under our noses.

GUARD YOU MOUTH, STAY SAFE, AND HAVE WONDERFUL DAY.

"IN GOD WE TRUST"

OCTOBER 20

YOU ARE NOT CONDEMNED,

1 John 3:18-22

18 My little children, let us not love in word, neither in tongue; but in deed and in truth. 19 And hereby we know that we are of the truth, and shall assure our hearts before him. 20 For if our heart condemn us, God is greater than our heart, and knoweth all things. 21 Beloved, if our heart condemn us not, then have we confidence toward God. 22 And whatsoever we ask, we receive of him, because we keep his commandments, and do those things that are pleasing in his sight.

KJV

1 John 3:18-22

18 Little children, let us not love [merely] in theory or in speech but in deed and in truth (in practice and in sincerity). 19 By this we shall come to know (perceive, recognize, and understand) that we are of the Truth, and can reassure (quiet, conciliate, and pacify) our hearts in His presence, 20 Whenever our hearts in [tormenting] self-accusation make us feel guilty and condemn us. [For we are in God's hands.] For He is above and greater than our consciences (our hearts), and He knows (perceives and understands) everything [nothing is hidden from Him]. 21 And, beloved, if our consciences (our hearts) do not accuse us [if they do not make us feel guilty and condemn us], we have confidence (complete assurance and boldness) before God, 22 And we receive from Him whatever we ask, because we [watchfully] obey His orders [observe His suggestions and injunctions, follow His plan for us] and [habitually] practice what is pleasing to Him. AMP

As we go through the day we are afforded many opportunities to show the love of God to others. As we see a person in need we can stop and help or ignore the situation. Their gratitude, is our reward from them. God sees our works and from Him we have great rewards. The need you see could be many things, loneliness, money, physical help, etc. When you see or know of a need, don't ignore God's call to your heart to help. Your reward will be great. Never have I seen such a display of these scriptures being fulfilled as in world war two, and the aftermath of the September the eleventh disaster. And now as we support

our troops in prayer, "that are fighting to keep our country and us safe from terrorists", let us do so with God's love flowing through us, then we can,.

ASK AND RECEIVE, HAVE A GREAT DAY

"IN GOD WE TRUST"

Pastor Ray

OCTOBER 21

YOU ARE GOD'S FRIEND

John 15:15-17

15 Henceforth I call you not servants; for the servant knoweth not what his lord doeth: but I have called you friends; for all things that I have heard of my Father I have made known unto you. **16** Ye have not chosen me, but I have chosen you, and ordained you, that ye should go and bring forth fruit, and that your fruit should remain: that whatsoever ye shall ask of the Father in my name, he may give it you. **17** These things I command you, that ye love one another. KJV

John 15:15-17

15 I do not call you servants (slaves) any longer, for the servant does not know what his master is doing (working out). But I have called you My friends, because I have made known to you everything that I have heard from My Father. [I have revealed to you everything that I have learned from Him.] 16 You have not chosen Me, but I have chosen you and I have appointed you [I have planted you], that you might go and bear fruit and keep on bearing, and that your fruit may be lasting [that it may remain, abide], so that whatever you ask the Father in My Name [as presenting all that I AM], He may give it to you. 17 This is what I command you: that you love one another. AMP

Isn't it good to know that we have a good friend in the heavenly Father that loves us and wants to give us His best. If we will produce the fruit of the Spirit in our lives then He will do His part to fulfill this promise. and give us what we ask for, that is in line with His Word, Think like God, ask and receive.

BE BLESSED, AND HAVE A GREAT DAY.

"IN GOD WE TRUST"

Pastor Ray

OCTOBER 22

YOU HAVE SOMEONE WATCHING OVER YOU

Ps 23:1-4

The Lord is my shepherd; I shall not want. **2** He maketh me to lie down in green pastures: he leadeth me beside the still waters. **3** He restoreth my soul: he leadeth me in the paths of righteousness for his name's sake. **4** Yea, though I walk through the valley of the shadow of death, I will fear no evil: for thou art with me; thy rod and thy staff they comfort me KJV

Ps 23:1-4

1 THE LORD is my Shepherd [to feed, guide, and shield me], I shall not lack. 2 He makes me lie down in [fresh, tender] green pastures; He leads me beside the still and restful waters. 3 He refreshes and restores my life (my self); He leads me in the paths of righteousness [uprightness and right standing with Him—not for my earning it, but] for His name's sake. 4 Yes, though I walk through the [deep, sunless] valley of the shadow of death, I will fear or dread no evil, for You are with me; Your rod [to protect] and Your staff [to guide], they comfort me. AMP

This is very special and personal for you, as you read notice the words, my, I, and, me, as you read, say the words out loud, and you will hear yourself speaking to yourself through your inner ear, and you will believe yourself, before you will believe anyone else.

HEAR AND KNOW WHO GOD IS, AND WHOM HE IS WATCHING OVER, HAVE A GREAT AND PROSPEROUS DAY.

"IN GOD WE TRUST"

OCTOBER 23

GOD KNOWS YOUR INTENTIONS

Prov 24:10-12

10 If thou faint in the day of adversity, thy strength is small. **11** If thou forbear to deliver them that are drawn unto death, and those that are ready to be slain; **12** If thou sayest, Behold, we knew it not; doth not he that pondereth the heart consider it? and he that keepeth thy soul, doth not he know it? and shall not he render to every man according to his works? KJV

Prov 24:10-12

10 If you falter in times of trouble, how small is your strength! 11 Rescue those being led away to death; hold back those staggering toward slaughter. 12 If you say, "But we knew nothing about this," does not he who weighs the heart perceive it? Does not he who guards your life know it? Will he not repay each person according to what he has done? NIV

God knows our hearts and every thought we have, He is watching over us to keep us strong and available to help in times of need. God will not force you to do something you do not want to do, and the devil can not make you do anything you do not want to do, so lean on the strong arm of God and be ready to respond to His call. He knows your heart and intentions.

BE STRONG AND READY, AND HAVE A NICE DAY.

"IN GOD WE TRUST"

Pastor Ray

OCTOBER 24

THIS IS YOUR DAY

Ps 118:21-25

21 I will praise thee: for thou hast heard me, and art become my salvation. **22** The stone which the builders refused is become the head stone of the corner. **23** This is the Lord's doing; it is marvellous in our eyes. **24** This is the day which the Lord hath made; we will rejoice and be glad in it. **25** Save now, I beseech thee, O Lord: O Lord, I beseech thee, send now prosperity. KJV

Ps 118:21-25

21 I will confess, praise, and give thanks to You, for You have heard and answered me; and You have become my Salvation and Deliverer. 22 The stone which the builders rejected has become the chief cornerstone. 23 This is from the Lord and is His doing; it is marvelous in our eyes. 24 This is the day which the Lord has brought about; we will rejoice and be glad in it. 25 Save now, we beseech You, O Lord; send now prosperity, O Lord, we beseech You, and give to us success! AMP

Every day is the day He has made and we should expect great things from Him. We can rejoice in the gifts we receive from Him, from the little ones like a good parking space in a crowded lot, or an auto air conditioner repair that only cost nine cents and took less than 5 minutes, or a major thing like good health, salvation, the restoration of a relationship, or financial needs met. For this is a day He has made for us to be glad and rejoice in.

PURPOSE IN YOUR HEART AND MIND TO REJOICE, AND HAVE A *GREAT DAY.*

"IN GOD WE TRUST"

OCTOBER 25

GOD'S PROMISES ARE HIS GIFTS TO YOU

2 Cor 1:20, Rom 11:29, 3 John 2

20 For all the promises of God in him are yea, and in him Amen, unto the glory of God by us. 29 for God's gifts and his call are irrevocable. 3 John 2 Beloved, I wish above all things that thou mayest prosper and be in health, even as thy soul prospereth. KJV

2 Cor 1:20, Rom 11:29, 3 John 2

20 For as many as are the promises of God, they all find their Yes [answer] in Him [Christ]. For this reason we also utter the Amen (so be it) to God through Him [in His Person and by His agency] to the glory of God. 29 For God's gifts and His call are irrevocable. [He never withdraws them when once they are given, and He does not change His mind about those to whom He gives His grace or to whom He sends His call.] 2 Beloved, I pray that you may prosper in every way and [that your body] may keep well, even as [I know] your soul keeps well and prospers. AMP

God never makes a promise that He does not intend to keep, and what He gives He will not take away from us. He has given us the measure of faith with which we can believe Him for what His word says, and believe His promises are true and for us today. Beloved (that's you) I wish for you to prosper and be in good health.

RECEIVE GOD'S PROMISES, AND HAVE A GREAT DAY.

"IN GOD WE TRUST"

Pastor Ray

OCTOBER 26

YOUR NEED IS MET

Phil 4:19-20

19 But my God shall supply all your need according to his riches in glory by Christ Jesus. **20** Now unto God and our Father be glory for ever and ever. Amen. KJV

Phil 4:19-20

19 And this same God who takes care of me will supply all your needs from his glorious riches, which have been given to us in Christ Jesus. 20 Now all glory to God our Father forever and ever! Amen.

Holy Bible, New Living Translation ®, copyright © 1996, 2004 by Tyndale Charitable Trust. Used by permission of Tyndale House Publishers. All rights reserved.

God is faithful to keep His word, and His Word says that my God shall supply all your need, that's right my God, the God I serve has promised according to his Word to supply all your need according to His riches in glory by Christ Jesus, and God is not one who lies. He also promised where two are agreed on earth as touching anything they shall ask that it would be done for them (Mat 18:19) So let us get in agreement as touching our needs and the needs of our nation that they shall be met by our Father Which is in Heaven, whether they are physical, financial or Spiritual, and especially guidance as we go through these rough times and as we go to the poles to vote this next election day.

AMEN, SO BE IT. HAVE A GREAT DAY

"IN GOD WE TRUST"

OCTOBER 27

YOU ARE NEVER ALONE

Haggai 2:4

4 Yet now be strong, O Zerubbabel, saith the LORD; and be strong, O Joshua, son of Josedech, the high priest; and be strong, all ye people of the land, saith the LORD, and work: for I am with you, saith the LORD of hosts: KJV

Hag 2:4-5

4 But now the Lord says: Be strong, Zerubbabel. Be strong, Jeshua son of Jehozadak, the high priest. Be strong, all you people still left in the land. And now get to work, for I am with you, says the Lord of Heaven's Armies.

Holy Bible, New Living Translation ®, copyright © 1996, 2004 by Tyndale Charitable Trust. Used by permission of Tyndale House Publishers. All rights reserved.

This is for you today, your name may not be Zerubbabel, or Joshua, but you can put your name in there or just be one of the people of the land. His Word is just as true for us today as it was then, He also promised He would never leave us or forsake us, so we can rest assured that He is with us wherever we go and whatever we do. Rest assured that He will bring us through this with VICTORY.

IN HIM WE HAVE THE VICTORY, HAVE A VICTORIOUS AND HAPPY DAY

"IN GOD WE TRUST"

OCTOBER 28

DON'T BE AFRAID, GOD HAS A GIFT FOR YOU, PEACE

John 14:25-27

25 These things have I spoken unto you, being yet present with you. **26** But the Comforter, which is the Holy Ghost, whom the Father will send in my name, he shall teach you all things, and bring all things to your remembrance, whatsoever I have said unto you. **27** Peace I leave with you, my peace I give unto you: not as the world giveth, give I unto you. Let not your heart be troubled, neither let it be afraid. KJV

John 14:25-27

25 I have told you these things while I am still with you. 26 But the Comforter (Counselor, Helper, Intercessor, Advocate, Strengthener, Standby), the Holy Spirit, Whom the Father will send in My name [in My place, to represent Me and act on My behalf], He will teach you all things. And He will cause you to recall (will remind you of, bring to your remembrance) everything I have told you. 27 Peace I leave with you; My [own] peace I now give and bequeath to you. Not as the world gives do I give to you. Do not let your hearts be troubled, neither let them be afraid. [Stop allowing yourselves to be agitated and disturbed; and do not permit yourselves to be fearful and intimidated and cowardly and unsettled.] AMP

When we have received this gift of God (Peace beyond understanding), there is nothing that should cause us to worry or be afraid of what may come, His peace lets us know that He is able to carry us through the toughest times.

LET GOD GUIDE YOU, AND HAVE A GREAT DAY.

"IN GOD WE TRUST"

OCTOBER 29

PUT YOUR TRUST IN GOD AND BE SAFE

Prov 29:25-27

25 The fear of man bringeth a snare: but whoso putteth his trust in the Lord shall be safe. **26** Many seek the ruler's favour; but every man's judgment cometh from the Lord. **27** An unjust man is an abomination to the just: and he that is upright in the way is abomination to the wicked. KJV

Prov 29:25-27

25 The fear of man brings a snare, but whoever leans on, trusts in, and puts his confidence in the Lord is safe and set on high. 26 Many crave and seek the ruler's favor, but the wise man [waits] for justice from the Lord. 27 An unjust man is an abomination to the righteous, and he who is upright in the way [of the Lord] is an abomination to the wicked. AMP

God is good all the time, He never changes, His judgment will be the same next week as it is today, so we can rest assured that if we turn to Him we will be safe, the choice is ours, walk with Him safely, or stumble along on our own.

STAY RIGHT WITH GOD, LET HIM LEAD, AND YOU HAVE A GREAT DAY.

"IN GOD WE TRUST"

Pastor Ray

OCTOBER 30

BE NOT AFRAID

Deut 20:1-4

when thou goest out to battle against thine enemies, and seest horses, and chariots, and a people more than thou, be not afraid of them: for the Lord thy God is with thee, which brought thee up out of the land of Egypt. **2** And it shall be, when ye are come nigh unto the battle, that the priest shall approach and speak unto the people, **3** And shall say unto them, Hear, O Israel, ye approach this day unto battle against your enemies: let not your hearts faint, fear not, and do not tremble, neither be ye terrified because of them; **4** For the Lord your God is he that goeth with you, to fight for you against your enemies, to save you. KJV

Deut 20:1-4

1 WHEN YOU go forth to battle against your enemies and see horses and chariots and an army greater than your own, do not be afraid of them, for the Lord your God, Who brought you out of the land of Egypt, is with you. 2 And when you come near to the battle, the priest shall approach and speak to the men, 3 And shall say to them, Hear, O Israel, you draw near this day to battle against your enemies. Let not your [minds and] hearts faint; fear not, and do not tremble or be terrified [and in dread] because of them. 4 For the Lord your God is He Who goes with you to fight for you against your enemies to save you. AMP

As you go out today to face the world and the evil forces that are trying to take God out of everything. Do not be afraid to put your trust and faith in God, for He is with you through every trial, battle and circumstance. He is with you every step of the way.

HOLD ON, DON'T LET FEAR STOP YOU, HAVE A GREAT DAY.

"IN GOD WE TRUST"

Pastor Ray

OCTOBER 31

YOU HAVE OVERCOME

1 John 4:4-6

4 Ye are of God, little children, and have overcome them: because greater is he that is in you, than he that is in the world. **5** They are of the world: therefore speak they of the world, and the world heareth them. **6** We are of God: he that knoweth God heareth us; he that is not of God heareth not us. Hereby know we the spirit of truth, and the spirit of error. KJV

1 John 4:4-6

4 Little children, you are of God [you belong to Him] and have [already] defeated and overcome them [the agents of the antichrist], because He Who lives in you is greater (mightier) than he who is in the world. 5 They proceed from the world and are of the world; therefore it is out of the world [its whole economy morally considered] that they speak, and the world listens (pays attention) to them. 6 We are [children] of God. Whoever is learning to know God [progressively to perceive, recognize, and understand God by observation and experience, and to get an ever-clearer knowledge of Him] listens to us; and he who is not of God does not listen or pay attention to us. By this we know (recognize) the Spirit of Truth and the spirit of error. AMP

You are a child of God if you have accepted the Lord Jesus as your savior, thus you are an overcomer, notice the words have overcome, which is past tense, which means it has been done already, because the Lord Jesus Christ the anointed one, the greater one is resident in you, and has already defeated the enemies of Christ, so therefore you in Christ have the victory to go to the church of your choice, pray for guidance and go.

ENJOY YOUR VICTORY, AND HAVE A GREAT AND HAPPY DAY.

"IN GOD WE TRUST"

NOVEMBER 1

YOU ARE BLESSED

Ps 1:1-3

Blessed is the man that walketh not in the counsel of the ungodly, nor standeth in the way of sinners, nor sitteth in the seat of the scornful. **2** But his delight is in the law of the Lord; and in his law doth he meditate day and night. **3** And he shall be like a tree planted by the rivers of water, that bringeth forth his fruit in his season; his leaf also shall not wither; and whatsoever he doeth shall prosper. KJV

God says we are blessed, when we meet the requirements He has set forth for us, to walk in His ways, being obedient to His word, letting others see Jesus in us.

WALK WITH JESUS AND BE BLESSED, HAVE A GREAT DAY.

"IN GOD WE TRUST"

Pastor Ray

NOVEMBER 2

HOW TO GET YOUR PRAYERS ANSWERED

John 15:5-7

5 I am the vine, ye are the branches: He that abideth in me, and I in him, the same bringeth forth much fruit: for without me ye can do nothing. **6** If a man abide not in me, he is cast forth as a branch, and is withered; and men gather them, and cast them into the fire, and they are burned. **7** If ye abide in me, and my words abide in you, ye shall ask what ye will, and it shall be done unto you. KJV

When we put God and His Word first place in our lives, and truly believe what He says in His word (the Bible), then we will receive because we believe. Fill yourself with His Word, stay hooked up to Him, this is the way we abide in Him, and by being full of His Word He abides in us, and our prayers will be answered.

Let us all pray and believe that God remains in charge of our Nation and selects the right people to guide us into the future.

PRAY, BELIEVE, AND RECEIVE. HAVE A WONDERFUL DAY.

"IN GOD WE TRUST"

NOVEMBER 3

DO YOU WANT TO FIND FAVOR?

Prov 3:3-4

3 Let not mercy and truth forsake thee: bind them about thy neck; write them upon the table of thine heart: **4** So shalt thou find favour and good understanding in the sight of God and man. KJV

Let love and truth be your guide as you go through your time here on earth. Let people see Jesus in you so that God can draw them to Himself through you.

WALK IN LOVE, AND BE LOVED. HAVE A GREAT DAY.

"IN GOD WE TRUST"

Pastor Ray

NOVEMBER 4

YOU HAVE HELP WITH YOUR CARES

1 Peter 5:6-7

6 Humble yourselves therefore under the mighty hand of God, that he may exalt you in due time: **7** Casting all your care upon him; for he careth for you. KJV

Let God help us through our trials and troubles, let us go to Him in prayer making our need known to Him, then leave them there with Him, for He loves us and cares for us and our Nation as well. He gives us directions on how to keep our Country well in 2 Chronicles 7:14, If my people, which are called by my name, shall humble themselves, and pray, and seek my face, and turn from their wicked ways; then will I hear from heaven, and will forgive their sin, and will heal their land. KJV.

HUMBLE YOURSELF AND PRAY. HAVE A PEACEFUL AND JOYOUS DAY.

"IN GOD WE TRUST"

Pastor Ray

NOVEMBER 5

PRAY, GOD WILL LISTEN

Ps 5:1-4

Give ear to my words, O Lord, consider my meditation. **2** Hearken unto the voice of my cry, my King, and my God: for unto thee will I pray. **3** My voice shalt thou hear in the morning, O Lord; in the morning will I direct my prayer unto thee, and will look up. **4** For thou art not a God that hath pleasure in wickedness: neither shall evil dwell with thee. KJV

God will hear our prayers, He heard us when we asked Jesus to come in and take charge of our lives, if He heard that cry for help, when we were out in the world alone, how much more will God hear our prayers now, but remember that he uses people to answer them, God used Moses to set His people free, God told Moses what to do at the burning bush, and sent him forth to answer the prayers of his people in Egypt to be free, and He will answer your prayers through someone.

CAN GOD USE YOU? HAVE A PRAYERFUL HAPPY DAY

"IN GOD WE TRUST"

Pastor Ray

NOVEMBER 6

GOD IS ON YOUR SIDE

Rom 8:31-32

31 What shall we then say to these things? If God be for us, who can be against us? **32** He that spared not his own Son, but delivered him up for us all, how shall he not with him also freely give us all things? KJV

When God is for us we have an army of His angels around us to see that we are protected. Our part is to rest assured that God means what He says, have faith in Him, and know that He is able to stand behind His Word to perform it.

GOD WILL PERFORM HIS WORD, RELAX, AND HAVE A NICE DAY

"IN GOD WE TRUST"

Pastor Ray

November 7

DO YOU WANT TO LIVE?

Prov 7:1-4

My son, keep my words, and lay up my commandments with thee. 2 Keep my commandments, and live; and my law as the apple of thine eye.

3 Bind them upon thy fingers, write them upon the table of thine heart. 4 Say unto wisdom, Thou art my sister; and call understanding thy kinswoman: KJV

Prov 7:1-4

1 MY SON, keep my words; lay up within you my commandments [for use when needed] and treasure them. 2 Keep my commandments and live, and keep my law and teaching as the apple (the pupil) of your eye. 3 Bind them on your fingers; write them on the tablet of your heart. 4 Say to skillful and godly Wisdom, You are my sister, and regard understanding or insight as your intimate friend—AMP

Do you really want to live a good life?, then follow God's instructions, study His Word [the Bible] to find out what wisdom is, and the way He wants you to use it. God wants to bless you abundantly, He is with you every day of your life, he knows you better than you know yourself, His word tells us in [Jer 29:11, AMP] For I know the thoughts and plans that I have for you, says the Lord, thoughts and plans for welfare and peace and not for evil, to give you hope in your final outcome.

PRAY, STUDY, LISTEN TO GOD, AND HAVE A GOOD LIFE, ALSO A GREAT DAY TODAY.

"IN GOD WE TRUST"

NOVEMBER 8

GOD HAS CHOSEN YOU

1 Corinthians 6:19-20

19 What? know ye not that your body is the temple of the Holy Ghost which is in you, which ye have of God, and ye are not your own? 20 For ye are bought with a price: therefore glorify God in your body, and in your spirit, which are God's.

The King James Version, (Cambridge: Cambridge) 1769.

The Holy Spirit of God has been given to you to give you power to be a witness for him, also to give you power to go through every situation you are faced with, to give you strength to overcome, to make you the head and not the tail, to place you above and not beneath.

LET PEOPLE SEE JESUS IN YOU. HAVE A GREAT DAY.

"IN GOD WE TRUST"

November 9

SEEK WISDOM, AND LIVE LONG AND WELL

Prov 9:9-12

9 Give instruction to a wise man, and he will be yet wiser: teach a just man, and he will increase in learning. **10** The fear of the Lord is the beginning of wisdom: and the knowledge of the holy is understanding. **11** For by me thy days shall be multiplied, and the years of thy life shall be increased. **12** If thou be wise, thou shalt be wise for thyself: but if thou scornest, thou alone shalt bear it. KJV

The scriptures tell us to diligently seek God and we shall find Him, (Jer 29:13 And ye shall seek me, and find me, when ye shall search for me with all your heart.) When we receive Jesus as the Lord of our lives, that is the beginning of our training, or wisdom and knowledge, and when we have finished our training we will be sent forth to share what we have learned with others. Study to show your self approved.

GO FORTH, BE BLESSED, AND HAVE A GREAT DAY

"IN GOD WE TRUST"

Pastor Ray

NOVEMBER 10

YOU HAVE OVERCOME

1 John 4:1-4

Beloved, believe not every spirit, but try the spirits whether they are of God: because many false prophets are gone out into the world. **2** Hereby know ye the Spirit of God: Every spirit that confesseth that Jesus Christ is come in the flesh is of God: **3** And every spirit that confesseth not that Jesus Christ is come in the flesh is not of God: and this is that spirit of antichrist, whereof ye have heard that it should come; and even now already is it in the world. **4** Ye are of God, little children, and have overcome them: because greater is he that is in you, than he that is in the world. KJV

You are a child of God if you have accepted the Lord Jesus as your savor, thus you have overcome the wicked ones, notice the word have, which is past tense, which means it has been done already, because the Lord Jesus Christ the anointed, the greater one is resident in you.

HOLD FAST TO YOUR CONFESSION OF CHRIST, IT IS YOUR LIFELINE.

"IN GOD WE TRUST"

Pastor Ray

November 11

REJECT FEAR

2 Timothy 1:7

7 For God hath not given us the spirit of fear; but of power, and of love, and of a sound mind. KJV

2 Tim 1:7

7 For the Spirit which God has given us is not a spirit of cowardice, but one of power and of love and of sound judgement. Weymouth

Reject fear, it is not a gift from God, but from the enemy. Take your gift of faith and power resist or reject fear and it will not control you. When fear knocks at your door, let your faith answer and there will be no one there. Your gift from God is power, love and a sound mind, NOT FEAR.

PRAY FOR OUR NATION, AND OUR TROOP'S THAT DEFEND US, AND OUR VETERANS, HAVE A GREAT DAY

"IN GOD WE TRUST"

NOVEMBER 12

ANGER IS HARMFUL

James 1:19-21

19 Wherefore, my beloved brethren, let every man be swift to hear, slow to speak, slow to wrath: **20** For the wrath of man worketh not the righteousness of God. **21** Wherefore lay apart all filthiness and superfluity of naughtiness, and receive with meekness the engrafted word, which is able to save your souls. KJV

Anger is first of all harmful to you, and then to all around you, It will destroy relationships and cause you great sorrow for the words you have spoken. Determine in your heart not to let the sun go down on your wrath. My wife and I made that decision sixty six years ago, and we believe it has played a big part in our marriage lasting all those years. We decided to not go to sleep angry at each other, oh there were a few long nights mostly in the first two years, but not many, and none since then. And there will be no chance of any more, since she went home to be with the Lord five years and four months ago. What a great life we had.

BE KIND TO EACH OTHER. IN EVERY RELATIONSHIP WHILE THERE IS TIME. HAVE A GREAT DAY.

"IN GOD WE TRUST"

NOVEMBER 13

KEEP YOUR HOPE UP

Prov 13:11-12

11 Wealth gotten by vanity shall be diminished: but he that gathereth by labour shall increase.
12 Hope deferred maketh the heart sick: but when the desire cometh, it is a tree of life. KJV

Hope is the blue print of what we are believing for, and when we begin to give up or hope it is like a blue print that the lines have started to fade and you are no longer able to make out the desired object. It is like when our vision is blurred, we are hoping for something that we do not have a clear picture of inside of us.

KEEP YOUR HOPE UP, YOUR VISION SHARP UNTIL YOU HAVE RECEIVED WHAT YOU ARE HOPING FOR. DON'T GIVE UP ON GOD, HE NEVER GAVE UP ON YOU.

THEN LET YOUR JOY OVERFLOW.

"IN GOD WE TRUST"

Pastor Ray

NOVEMBER 14

WALK WITH GOD!

Prov 14:10-13

The heart knoweth his own bitterness; and a stranger doth not intermeddle with his joy. 11 The house of the wicked shall be overthrown: but the tabernacle of the upright shall flourish. 12 There is a way which seemeth right unto a man, but the end thereof are the ways of death. 13 Even in laughter the heart is sorrowful; and the end of that mirth is heaviness. KJV

Let God hold you hand, and walk close to Him, He knows the thoughts and plans He has for you, plans for good, not for evil, plans to bring you to your expected end with Him, hold on tight, don't let your good future slip away, His way will bring you joyfully into His kingdom to spend eternity with Him in Heaven.

LET GOD LEAD YOU TO YOUR DESTINATION. HAVE A GREAT DAY.

"IN GOD WE TRUST"

Pastor Ray

November 15

RUN TO GOD

Proverbs 18:10

10 The name of the LORD is a strong tower: the righteous runneth into it, and is safe.

The King James Version, (Cambridge: Cambridge) 1769.

Prov 18:10

10 The name of the Lord is a strong tower; the [consistently] righteous man [upright and in right standing with God] runs into it and is safe, high [above evil] *and* strong. AMP

God always has his arm outstretched for us to run into, He loves to be able to put His arms around us and comfort us when we need help, no matter what the problem may be. We should always run to Him and not away from, as He is always there waiting for us to make the move towards Him. It is your turn.

RUN TO GOD, DON'T LOOK BACK, AND HAVE A GREAT DAY WITH HIM.

"IN GOD WE TRUST"

Pastor Ray

NOVEMBER 16

GOD WANTS YOU TO HAVE A GOOD LIFE

Proverbs 21:21

21 He that followeth after righteousness and mercy findeth life, righteousness, and honour.

The King James Version, (Cambridge: Cambridge) 1769.

We are told in Proverbs 3:1-2 (AMP) that if we keep His commandments we will have a long life worth living, that means with peace, Love, righteousness, and honor, finding favor with God and man.

WHAT A GREAT PLACE TO BE. HAVE A GREAT DAY

"IN GOD WE TRUST"

Pastor Ray

November 17

GOD'S COVENANT PROMISES ARE FOR YOU

Deut 8:17-18

17 And thou say in thine heart, My power and the might of mine hand hath gotten me this wealth. **18** But thou shalt remember the Lord thy God: for it is he that giveth thee power to get wealth, that he may establish his covenant which he sware unto thy fathers, as it is this day. KJV

With a promise like this how can we begin to think that God does not want us to be prosperous in every area of our life. Even though the covenant was made with our ancestors, it is for us this day, so receive the power to get wealth and put it to work in your life. It is your heritage, but remember who gave it to you. The purpose of this gift is to establish His covenant with you this very day.

DON'T RESIST, HAVE A BEAUTIFUL AND HAPPY DAY.

"IN GOD WE TRUST"

NOVEMBER 18

GODS GIFT TO YOU, HEALTH

1 Peter 2:24

24 Who his own self bare our sins in his own body on the tree, that we, being dead to sins, should live unto righteousness: by whose stripes ye were healed.

The King James Version, (Cambridge: Cambridge) 1769.

1 Peter 2:24

24 He personally bore our sins in His [own] body on the tree, [as on an altar and offered Himself on it], that we might die (cease to exist) to sin and live to righteousness. By His wounds you have been healed. AMP

Notice the words were and have, they are both past tense which means that you already have been healed and health is yours. Don't let anyone steal from you what is yours, it is paid for and given to you. Fight to keep it. It is like having money in the bank and refusing to write a check when you are hungry and don't have the cash on hand to buy food.

BE BLESSED, AND ENJOY YOUR DAY

"IN GOD WE TRUST"

Pastor Ray

NOVEMBER 19

IS ANYTHING TO HARD FOR GOD?

Gen 18:13-14

13 And the Lord said unto Abraham, Wherefore did Sarah laugh, saying, Shall I of a surety bear a child, which am old? **14** Is any thing too hard for the Lord? At the time appointed I will return unto thee, according to the time of life, and Sarah shall have a son. KJV

If God can work this kind of miracle with a couple in there 90s, then surely our problems are a simple task for Him, but we have to give them to Him before He can do anything with them. We can not take them back in a short time because we think He is not working fast enough, remember He is working with people.

PEOPLE ARE NOT ALWAYS OBEDIENT. OBEY, AND HAVE A GREAT DAY.

"IN GOD WE TRUST"

Pastor Ray

NOVEMBER 20

BE NOT AFRAID

Ps 27:1-3

The Lord is my light and my salvation; whom shall I fear? the Lord is the strength of my life; of whom shall I be afraid? **2** When the wicked, even mine enemies and my foes, came upon me to eat up my flesh, they stumbled and fell. **3** Though an host should encamp against me, my heart shall not fear: though war should rise against me, in this will I be confident. KJV

Prov 27:1-3

1 DO NOT boast of [yourself and] tomorrow, for you know not what a day may bring forth. 2 Let another man praise you, and not your own mouth; a stranger, and not your own lips. 3 Stone is heavy and sand weighty, but a fool's [unreasoning] wrath is heavier and more intolerable than both of them. AMP

Don't let your heart be troubled, and be not afraid, for God is on your side and He has won the victory. Fear is not for you, God has not given you a Spirit of fear, that's of the devil. We are told in 2 Tim 1:7 For God did not give us a spirit of timidity (of cowardice, of craven and cringing and fawning fear), but [He has given us a spirit] of power and of love and of calm and well-balanced mind and discipline and self-control. AMP

YOU WIN, STAY COOL, AND HAVE A GREAT DAY.

"IN GOD WE TRUST"

Pastor Ray

NOVEMBER 21

GOD DOES NOT WANT YOU IN THIS POSITION

Prov 21:17-18

17 He that loveth pleasure shall be a poor man: he that loveth wine and oil shall not be rich. **18** The wicked shall be a ransom for the righteous, and the transgressor for the upright. KJV

God wants you in a position to hear Him and do what is right and share His word with others, His desire for you is health and prosperity, 3 John 2 Beloved, I wish above all things that thou mayest prosper and be in health, even as thy soul prospereth. Jer. 29:11 For I know the thoughts that I think toward you, saith the Lord, thoughts of peace, and not of evil, to give you an expected end. KJV

LET GOD HAVE HIS WAY, HAVE A GREAT WEEK.

"IN GOD WE TRUST"

Pastor Ray

NOVEMBER 22

YOU ARE SPECIAL

John 15:16

16 Ye have not chosen me, but I have chosen you, and ordained you, that ye should go and bring forth fruit, and that your fruit should remain: that whatsoever ye shall ask of the Father in my name, he may give it you. KJV

Isn't it good to know that we have a heavenly Father that loves us and wants to give us His best. If we will produce the fruit of the Spirit in our lives then He will do His part to fulfill this promise.

BE BLESSED, AND HAVE A GOOD DAY.

"IN GOD WE TRUST"

Pastor Ray

NOVEMBER 23

HAVE FAITH IN GOD

Mark 11:22-26

22 And Jesus answering saith unto them, Have faith in God. **23** For verily I say unto you, That whosoever shall say unto this mountain, Be thou removed, and be thou cast into the sea; and shall not doubt in his heart, but shall believe that those things which he saith shall come to pass; he shall have whatsoever he saith. **24** Therefore I say unto you, What things soever ye desire, when ye pray, believe that ye receive them, and ye shall have them. **25** And when ye stand praying, forgive, if ye have ought against any: that your Father also which is in heaven may forgive you your trespasses. **26** But if ye do not forgive, neither will your Father which is in heaven forgive your trespasses. KJV

We have all received a measure of faith. Jesus is the author and finisher of our faith, but the exercising and developing of a strong faith is left up to us. If we never use our faith it will remain just the measure we started with, but if we exercise and train and work our faith it will become strong and productive, God will help us with it if we have faith in Him, for faith works by love and God is love. Build your faith to full strength that it may remove the mountains in your life, whatever they are.

HAVE THE FAITH OF GOD, AND HAVE A GREAT DAY.

"IN GOD WE TRUST"

Pastor Ray

November 24

AFTER A NIGHT OF TEARS, JOY COMES IN THE MORNING

Ps 30:4-5

4 Sing unto the Lord, O ye saints of his, and give thanks at the remembrance of his holiness. **5** For his anger endureth but a moment; in his favour is life: weeping may endure for a night, but joy cometh in the morning. KJV

God loves you, He wants to give you His shoulder to cry on, that He may dry your tears, and see you through the night, or dark times in your life, bringing you out into light and joy. Joy comes with the light as the night turns into day.

LET THE SON SHINE IN, AND HAVE A BRIGHT AND HAPPY WEEK, HAPPY THANKSGIVING.

"IN GOD WE TRUST"

NOVEMBER 25

HAPPY THANKSGIVING

Ps 95:1-3, 100:4-5

O come, let us sing unto the Lord: let us make a joyful noise to the rock of our salvation. **2** Let us come before his presence with thanksgiving, and make a joyful noise unto him with psalms. **3** For the Lord is a great God, and a great King above all gods. Ps 100:4-5 **4** Enter into his gates with thanksgiving, and into his courts with praise: be thankful unto him, and bless his name. **5** For the Lord is good; his mercy is everlasting; and his truth endureth to all generations. KJV

May you all have a Happy, safe and joyous Thanksgiving Holiday, as we enjoy the bountiful blessings He has given us.

BE BLESSED, AND HAVE A VERY HAPPY THANKSGIVING.

"IN GOD WE TRUST"

Pastor Ray

NOVEMBER 26

ABUNDANT LIFE IS YOURS

John 10:10

10 The thief cometh not, but for to steal, and to kill, and to destroy: I am come that they might have life, and that they might have it more abundantly.

The King James Version, (Cambridge: Cambridge) 1769.

Jesus came so we could live an abundant life, full of joy and peace. He also gave us the power to use His name to rebuke the destroyer, to keep him from stealing from us what God has given. Let us all enter into His rest with a grateful heart for what He has done, and retain that gratitude throughout the year.

BE THANKFUL TO GOD, AND HAVE A GREAT DAY

"IN GOD WE TRUST"

Pastor Ray

NOVEMBER 27

BE NOT AFRAID

Ps 27:1-3

The Lord is my light and my salvation; whom shall I fear? the Lord is the strength of my life; of whom shall I be afraid? **2** When the wicked, even mine enemies and my foes, came upon me to eat up my flesh, they stumbled and fell. **3** Though an host should encamp against me, my heart shall not fear: though war should rise against me, in this will I be confident. KJV

Don't let your heart be troubled, and be not afraid, for God is on your side and He has won the victory.

YOU WIN, STAY COOL, AND HAVE A GREAT DAY.

"IN GOD WE TRUST"

Pastor Ray

NOVEMBER 28

YOUR NEED IS MET

Phil 4:19-20

19 But my God shall supply all your need according to his riches in glory by Christ Jesus. **20** Now unto God and our Father be glory for ever and ever. Amen. KJV

God is able and willing to do what His Word declares, turn your need over to God in prayer, then in thanksgiving wait patiently for the manifestation. "Ps 100:4 Enter his gates with thanksgiving and his courts with praise; give thanks to him and praise his name." (NIV) God is faithful to do what He said He will do.

YOU ARE BLESSED. HAVE A GREAT DAY.

"IN GOD WE TRUST"

Pastor Ray

November 29

WITH GOD, YOU CAN HAVE HARMONY IN YOUR HOME

Prov 11:29

29 He that troubleth his own house shall inherit the wind: and the fool shall be servant to the wise of heart. KJV

Prov 11:29

29 He who troubles his own house shall inherit the wind, and the foolish shall be servant to the wise of heart. AMP

Do not be foolish, always put your soul mate first, right after God. Let God's love flow through you to those around you, and the response will be love coming back to you on a gentle breeze, rather than anger on a stiff wind. Have you ever tried to stand against a strong wind in a storm? It is a hard thing to do, it is better to lay down in a low place, and have it blow over you.

LOVE AND BE HAPPY, HAVE A GREAT DAY.

"IN GOD WE TRUST"

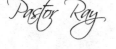

NOVEMBER 30

GETTING TIRED AND WORN OUT?

Isaiah 40:28-31(KJV)

28 Hast thou not known? hast thou not heard, that the everlasting God, the LORD, the Creator of the ends of the earth, fainteth not, neither is weary? there is no searching of his understanding. 29 He giveth power to the faint; and to them that have no might he increaseth strength. 30 Even the youths shall faint and be weary, and the young men shall utterly fall: 31 *But they that wait upon the LORD shall renew their strength;* they shall mount up with wings as eagles; they shall run, and not be weary; and they shall walk, and not faint.

What God wants us to know here is that no matter how tired and worn out we may get, He never tires or grows weary. If we will trust, believe and depend on Him to handle our situations and wait on Him, He will cause us to get new strength so that we can run and not get weary, walk and not faint, taking everything to Him in prayer and leaving it with Him. In other words let go and let God, don't take it back if you see no results in five seconds, trust Him, give Him time.

TURN IT OVER TO GOD, WAIT ON HIM, AND HAVE A RESTFUL AND PEACEFUL DAY.

"IN GOD WE TRUST"

Pastor Ray

DECEMBER 1

LISTEN TO GOD AND LIVE IN SAFETY

Prov 1:31-33

31 Therefore shall they eat of the fruit of their own way, and be filled with their own devices. **2** For the turning away of the simple shall slay them, and the prosperity of fools shall destroy them. **33** But whoso hearkeneth unto me shall dwell safely, and shall be quiet from fear of evil. KJV

Seek God and His wisdom, God's desire for those who have accepted Him, is for them to have wisdom, health, and safety. It is when we get out ahead of Him and have it our way that we loose sight of the wisdom that God has provided for us, and start making dumb decisions, and get on the path of destruction. God's Word gives us a strong warning in Hosea 4:6 My people are destroyed for lack of knowledge: because thou hast rejected knowledge, I will also reject thee, that thou shalt be no priest to me: seeing thou hast forgotten the law of thy God, I will also forget thy children.

STAY WITH GOD AND HIS WISDOM, AND KEEP YOUR CHILDREN SAFE, HAVE A GREAT DAY.

"IN GOD WE TRUST"

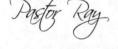

DECEMBER 2

LET GO AND LET GOD

Matt 5:43-48

43 Ye have heard that it hath been said, Thou shalt love thy neighbour, and hate thine enemy. **44** But I say unto you, Love your enemies, bless them that curse you, do good to them that hate you, and pray for them which despitefully use you, and persecute you; **45** That ye may be the children of your Father which is in heaven: for he maketh his sun to rise on the evil and on the good, and sendeth rain on the just and on the unjust. **46** For if ye love them which love you, what reward have ye? do not even the publicans the same? **47** And if ye salute your brethren only, what do ye more than others? do not even the publicans so? **48** Be ye therefore perfect, even as your Father which is in heaven is perfect.

KJV

If we will let go and pray for those who mistreat us and let God handle it, as He can do a much better job than you or I can, then His peace which passes all understanding will flood over you, as you realize that God loves you and is more than able to take care of your problems.

LET GO AND LET GOD, THEN ENJOY YOUR DAY.

"IN GOD WE TRUST"

DECEMBER 3

YOU ARE FORGIVEN

Ephesians 4:29-32

29 Let no corrupt communication proceed out of your mouth, but that which is good to the use of edifying, that it may minister grace unto the hearers. 30 And grieve not the holy Spirit of God, whereby ye are sealed unto the day of redemption. 31 Let all bitterness, and wrath, and anger, and clamour, and evil speaking, be put away from you, with all malice: 32 And be ye kind one to another, tenderhearted, forgiving one another, even as God for Christ's sake hath forgiven you.

The King James Version, (Cambridge: Cambridge) 1769.

Eph 4:29-32

29 Let no foul *or* polluting language, *nor* evil word *nor* unwholesome *or* worthless talk [ever] come out of your mouth, but only such [speech] as is good *and* beneficial to the spiritual progress of others, as is fitting to the need *and* the occasion, that it may be a blessing *and* give grace (God's favor) to those who hear it. **30** And do not grieve the Holy Spirit of God [do not offend or vex or sadden Him], by Whom you were sealed (marked, branded as God's own, secured) for the day of redemption (of final deliverance through Christ from evil and the consequences of sin). **31** Let all bitterness and indignation *and* wrath (passion, rage, bad temper) and resentment (anger, animosity) and quarreling (brawling, clamor, contention) and slander (evil-speaking, abusive or blasphemous language) be banished from you, with all malice (spite, ill will, or baseness of any kind). **32** And become useful *and* helpful *and* kind to one another, tenderhearted (compassionate, understanding, loving-hearted), forgiving one another [readily and freely], as God in Christ forgave you. AMP

Un-forgiveness will cause anger to be present in your heart, and out of the abundance of the heart your mouth speaks. Again let go and let God, forgive for you are forgiven. Notice the word hath and were, which are both past tense, which means it is already done, so receive it today.

YOU ARE FORGIVEN. HAVE A GREAT DAY.

"IN GOD WE TRUST"

DECEMBER 4

KEEP YOUR EYES ON THE RIGHT PATH

Prov 4:23-27

23 Keep thy heart with all diligence; for out of it are the issues of life. **24** Put away from thee a froward mouth, and perverse lips put far from thee. **25** Let thine eyes look right on, and let thine eyelids look straight before thee. **26** Ponder the path of thy feet, and let all thy ways be established. **27** Turn not to the right hand nor to the left: remove thy foot from evil. KJV

It is good to know that we have a God who will keep us on the right path, if we will only hold on and walk with Him, instead of going off on our own, and taking all those side trips out into the devils territory, risking our very lives for a few moments of what we think will be pleasure, and then have to pay the price and carry the scars.

STAY WITH GOD AND ENJOY YOUR DAY, AND THE JOURNEY THRU LIFE.

"IN GOD WE TRUST"

Pastor Ray

DECEMBER 5

REJOICE, THE BATTLE IS THE LORDS

Ps 5:11-12 KJV

11 But let all those that put their trust in thee rejoice: let them ever shout for joy, because thou defendest them: let them also that love thy name be joyful in thee. 12 For thou, Lord, wilt bless the righteous; with favour wilt thou compass him as with a shield.

Ps 5:11-12 NIV

11 But let all who take refuge in you be glad; let them ever sing for joy. Spread your protection over them, that those who love your name may rejoice in you. 12 For surely, O Lord, you bless the righteous; you surround them with your favor as with a shield.

God will protect you, He welcomes you with love and open arms, and will fight for you, He has a shield of protection around you, let you enemies know who they are fighting, let them see you dressed in Gods Armour and they will run for they know how bad Satan was beaten by the person wearing that Armour, keep your face plate closed and stand your ground. We are told in, 1 Sam 17:47 (KJV) And all this assembly shall know that the Lord saveth not with sword and spear: for the battle is the Lord's, and he will give you into our hands.

STICK WITH GOD AND WIN, AND HAVE A JOYFUL DAY.

"IN GOD WE TRUST"

DECEMBER 6

GOD SHALL SUPPLY YOUR NEED

Phil 4:19-20

19 But my God shall supply all your need according to his riches in glory by Christ Jesus. **20** Now unto God and our Father be glory for ever and ever. Amen. KJV

Phil 4:19-20

19 And my God will liberally supply (**o** fill to the full) your every need according to His riches in glory in Christ Jesus. **20** To our God and Father be glory forever and ever (through the endless eternities of the eternities). *Amen (so be it)*. AMP

Notice that the scripture says all of your need. God knows us better than we know ourselves, He knows all of our needs and will meet them when we decide to receive and get our selves into the right position with Him, by accepting Jesus as our Lord and savior and believing that He is the Son of God. Then pray and know that He hears us and grants the petitions we have laid before Him.

LET GOD HEAR YOUR PRAYERS, THEN EXPECT AN ANSWER.

"IN GOD WE TRUST"

Pastor Ray

DECEMBER 7

GOD WILL DRY YOUR TEARS

Rev 7:14-17

14 And I said unto him, Sir, thou knowest. And he said to me, These are they which came out of great tribulation, and have washed their robes, and made them white in the blood of the Lamb. 15 Therefore are they before the throne of God, and serve him day and night in his temple: and he that sitteth on the throne shall dwell among them. 16 They shall hunger no more, neither thirst any more; neither shall the sun light on them, nor any heat. 17 For the Lamb which is in the midst of the throne shall feed them, and shall lead them unto living fountains of waters: and God shall wipe away all tears from their eyes. KJV

If we will persevere in our walk with God until the end, we can rest in peace knowing that we shall spend eternity with Him, and have our every need met, Gods word tells us that our God shall supply all our need according to his riches in glory by Christ Jesus, here we are told that Jesus will be our shepherd, and that God will wipe away every tear.

LET GOD HAVE HIS WAY WITH YOU, AND ENJOY THE JOURNEY. HAVE A GREAT DAY

"IN GOD WE TRUST"

DECEMBER 8

GOOD THINGS ARE COMING YOUR WAY

Jer 29:11-13

11 For I know the thoughts that I think toward you, saith the Lord, thoughts of peace, and not of evil, to give you an expected end. **12** Then shall ye call upon me, and ye shall go and pray unto me, and I will hearken unto you. **13** And ye shall seek me, and find me, when ye shall search for me with all your heart. KJV

God shows His love toward us in many ways. The more we yield to Him the easier it is for Him to fulfill the plans He has for us, plans for good things, not bad.

SOMETHING GOOD IS GOING TO HAPPEN TO YOU.

"IN GOD WE TRUST"

Pastor Ray

DECEMBER 9

YOU ARE A VERY SPECIAL PERSON

Zeph 3:15-17

15 The Lord hath taken away thy judgments, he hath cast out thine enemy: the king of Israel, even the Lord, is in the midst of thee: thou shalt not see evil any more. **16** In that day it shall be said to Jerusalem, Fear thou not: and to Zion, Let not thine hands be slack. **17** The Lord thy God in the midst of thee is mighty; he will save, he will rejoice over thee with joy; he will rest in his love, he will joy over thee with singing. KJV

God has always loved you, even when you thought He did not know you existed. His heart is saddened when we get out from under His umbrella of protection, but he rejoices when we come back home to Him. So don't be afraid, or fearful. His love for you is never ending.

LET GO AND LET GOD. AND HAVE A GREAT DAY

"IN GOD WE TRUST"

Pastor Ray

DECEMBER 10

HOLD YOUR HEAD HIGH

Luke 21:25-28

25 And there shall be signs in the sun, and in the moon, and in the stars; and upon the earth distress of nations, with perplexity; the sea and the waves roaring; **26** Men's hearts failing them for fear, and for looking after those things which are coming on the earth: for the powers of heaven shall be shaken. **27** And then shall they see the Son of man coming in a cloud with power and great glory. **28** And when these things begin to come to pass, then look up, and lift up your heads; for your redemption draweth nigh. KJV

Is this the end times? It certainly sounds like today, with wars and rumors of wars, people wearing masks of protection, panic over all kind of things. We may ask what things? The day of the vengeance of the Lord. When we see these times we know that we should look up and hold our heads up for our redemption draweth neigh.

STAND FIRM, DON'T GIVE UP, HELP IS ON THE WAY.

"IN GOD WE TRUST"

Pastor Ray

DECEMBER 11

THE JOY OF THE LORD
IS YOUR STRENGTH

Nehemiah 8:10

10 Then he said unto them, Go your way, eat the fat, and drink the sweet, and send portions unto them for whom nothing is prepared: for this day is holy unto our Lord: neither be ye sorry; for the joy of the LORD is your strength.

The King James Version, (Cambridge: Cambridge) 1769.

Neh 8:10

10 Nehemiah said, "Go and enjoy choice food and sweet drinks, and send some to those who have nothing prepared. This day is sacred to our Lord. Do not grieve, for the joy of the Lord is your strength."

NIV

We are encouraged not to feel sorry for ourselves or be sad, but to celebrate with a feast of choice foods and sweet drinks (maybe a pot luck) and share with those who have nothing prepared, invite someone and tell them to bring nothing but themselves, for God gives us joy when we help others,

HIS JOY IS OUR STRENGTH, BE STRONG IN GOD, AND ENJOY YOUR DAY.

"IN GOD WE TRUST"

Pastor Ray

DECEMBER 12

FULLNESS OF JOY

Ps 16:8-11

8 I have set the Lord always before me: because he is at my right hand, I shall not be moved. **9** Therefore my heart is glad, and my glory rejoiceth: my flesh also shall rest in hope. **10** For thou wilt not leave my soul in hell; neither wilt thou suffer thine Holy One to see corruption. **11** Thou wilt shew me the path of life: in thy presence is fullness of joy; at thy right hand there are pleasures for evermore. KJV

Ps 16:8-11

8 I know the Lord is always with me. I will not be shaken, for he is right beside me. **9** No wonder my heart is glad, and I rejoice.* My body rests in safety. **10** For you will not leave my soul among the dead* or allow your holy one* to rot in the grave. **11** You will show me the way of life, granting me the joy of your presence and the pleasures of living with you forever.*

Holy Bible, New Living Translation ®, copyright © 1996, 2004 by Tyndale Charitable Trust. Used by permission of Tyndale House Publishers. All rights reserved.

This is the position God wants us to be in, close to Him, in His presence, so we can have fullness of joy and pleasure for evermore. He is our Father God and wishes to share our joy and pleasure, as our fullness of joy gives Him great pleasure.

STAY WITH GOD ON THE RIGHT PATH, AND REACH YOUR DESTINATION SAFELY.

"IN GOD WE TRUST"

DECEMBER 13

DO YOU WANT THE FAVOR OF GOD, AND A SURE WAY?

Prov 3:3-6

3 Let not mercy and truth forsake thee: bind them about thy neck; write them upon the table of thine heart: **4** So shalt thou find favour and good understanding in the sight of God and man. **5** Trust in the Lord with all thine heart; and lean not unto thine own understanding. **6** In all thy ways acknowledge him, and he shall direct thy paths.

KJV

Our problem is that most of the time we are the ones deciding which way to go and then want God to make the way easy. If we will only learn to trust Him, then hear where He wants us to go. We ask for directions, then go the opposite of what he tells us, He says go right at the fork in the road because He knows the bridge is out on the left road, but no we go left because we know it is the shortest way not knowing the bridge is out and that we will have to come all the back and then take the right road. John 14:6 Jesus saith unto him, I am the way, the truth, and the life: no man cometh unto the Father, but by me.(KJV)

OBEDIENCE IS BETTER THAN SACRIFICE, CHOOSE GOD'S WAY, AND HAVE A GREAT DAY.

"IN GOD WE TRUST"

DECEMBER 14

TAKE A BREAK

Hebrews 4:10-13

10 For he that is entered into his rest, he also hath ceased from his own works, as God did from his. 11 Let us labour therefore to enter into that rest, lest any man fall after the same example of unbelief. 12 For the word of God is quick, and powerful, and sharper than any twoedged sword, piercing even to the dividing asunder of soul and spirit, and of the joints and marrow, and is a discerner of the thoughts and intents of the heart. 13 Neither is there any creature that is not manifest in his sight: but all things are naked and opened unto the eyes of him with whom we have to do.

The King James Version, (Cambridge: Cambridge) 1769.

Entering into God's rest is easier said than done, we must put forth some effort, sincerely trying hard to hook up with Him and enter into His rest, a safe haven He has made for us, where we can put all of our cares over on Him, taking a break along with Him.

RELAX IN GOD, AND HAVE A GREAT WEEK

"IN GOD WE TRUST"

Pastor Ray

DECEMBER 15

THE WAY TO GOD'S PLACE

Ps 15

Lord, who shall abide in thy tabernacle? who shall dwell in thy holy hill? **2** He that walketh uprightly, and worketh righteousness, and speaketh the truth in his heart. **3** He that backbiteth not with his tongue, nor doeth evil to his neighbour, nor taketh up a reproach against his neighbour. **4** In whose eyes a vile person is contemned; but he honoureth them that fear the Lord. He that sweareth to his own hurt, and changeth not. **5** He that putteth not out his money to usury, nor taketh reward against the innocent. He that doeth these things shall never be moved. KJV

This Psalm needs no explanation, it is very clear as to how to get to live in God's tabernacle.

ENJOY THE TRIP.

"IN GOD WE TRUST"

Pastor Ray

DECEMBER 16

ARE YOU DRESSED FOR THE DAY?

Ephesians 6:13-19

13 Wherefore take unto you the whole armour of God, that ye may be able to withstand in the evil day, and having done all, to stand. 14 Stand therefore, having your loins girt about with truth, and having on the breastplate of righteousness; 15 And your feet shod with the preparation of the gospel of peace; 16 Above all, taking the shield of faith, wherewith ye shall be able to quench all the fiery darts of the wicked. 17 And take the helmet of salvation, and the sword of the Spirit, which is the word of God: 18 Praying always with all prayer and supplication in the Spirit, and watching thereunto with all perseverance and supplication for all saints;

The King James Version, (Cambridge: Cambridge) 1769.

When we are properly dressed with our full armor of God on, our shield of faith in one hand, and the sword of the Holy Spirit of God (The Bible) in the other, we are ready to stand against the wiles of the devil, quenching all of his fiery darts. You are aware that the only fiery darts that the devil has are thoughts. He has to have someone to take those thoughts, say them and act on them. It does not matter to him whether you are good or evil, he can do nothing without you.

TAKE NO THOUGHT SAYING, AND HAVE A SAFE AND HAPPY DAY

"IN GOD WE TRUST"

Pastor Ray

DECEMBER 17

SOWING AND REAPING

Gal 6:7-10

7 Be not deceived; God is not mocked: for whatsoever a man soweth, that shall he also reap. **8** For he that soweth to his flesh shall of the flesh reap corruption; but he that soweth to the Spirit shall of the Spirit reap life everlasting. **9** And let us not be weary in well doing: for in due season we shall reap, if we faint not. **10** As we have therefore opportunity, let us do good unto all men, especially unto them who are of the household of faith. KJV

God is no respecter of persons, His laws apply to us all. This scripture is assuring us that we will reap a harvest on what we sow, plant, or give out. If we want love, give love, if we want friendship, give friendship. We will reap a harvest on what we sow, good or bad. If we don't want to reap it, we had best not sow it.

SEED TIME & HARVEST TIME WILL ALWAYS BE. HAVE A GREAT DAY.

"IN GOD WE TRUST"

Pastor Ray

DECEMBER 18

GODS GIFT TO YOU, HEALTH

1 Peter 2:24

24 Who his own self bare our sins in his own body on the tree, that we, being dead to sins, should live unto righteousness: by whose stripes ye were healed.

The King James Version, (Cambridge: Cambridge) 1769.

1 Peter 2:24

24 He personally bore our sins in His [own] body on the tree, [as on an altar and offered Himself on it], that we might die (cease to exist) to sin and live to righteousness. By His wounds you have been healed. AMP

Notice the words were and have, they are both past tense which means that you already have been healed and health is yours. Don't let anyone steal from you what is yours, it is paid for and given to you. Fight to keep it. It is like having money in the bank and refusing to write a check when you are hungry and don't have the cash on hand to buy food.

BE BLESSED, AND ENJOY YOUR DAY

"IN GOD WE TRUST"

DECEMBER 19

GOD'S WORDS, AND LOVE IS FOR YOU

Ps 19:7-11

7 The law of the Lord is perfect, converting the soul: the testimony of the Lord is sure, making wise the simple. **8** The statutes of the Lord are right, rejoicing the heart: the commandment of the Lord is pure, enlightening the eyes. **9** The fear of the Lord is clean, enduring for ever: the judgments of the Lord are true and righteous altogether. **10** More to be desired are they than gold, yea, than much fine gold: sweeter also than honey and the honeycomb. **11** Moreover by them is thy servant warned: and in keeping of them there is great reward. KJV

Are you looking for hidden treasure? Then follow God's directions, and stay on the path He has laid out for you.

GOD'S WORD WARNS US OF DANGER, AND KEEPS US ON THE RIGHT PATH. HAVE A GREAT WEEK END.

"IN GOD WE TRUST"

DECEMBER 20

GOD HEARS YOUR CRY, EVERYTHING IS GOING TO BE ALL RIGHT

Ps 20:5-6

5 We will rejoice in your salvation, And in the name of our God we will set up *our* banners! May the Lord fulfill all your petitions. **6** Now I know that the Lord saves His anointed; He will answer him from His holy heaven With the saving strength of His right hand. NKJV

When you cry out to god for help, God hears you, and will send help, and grant you what you have prayed about, He only gives you what is good for you, which brings joy to your heart, a smile to your face, and prosperity in every area. When we see you rejoice, we will rejoice with you in your victory.

GODS LOVE FOR YOU IS NEVER ENDING.

"IN GOD WE TRUST"

Pastor Ray

DECEMBER 21

YOU ARE SAFE WITH GOD

Prov 21:30-31

30 There is no wisdom nor understanding nor counsel against the Lord. **31** The horse is prepared against the day of battle: but safety is of the Lord. KJV

Your safety and victory is in the Lord, don't try to accomplish it without Him, He is your protector, your guide, your salvation, your ever present helper.

HOLD TIGHTLY TO GOD, AND ENJOY YOUR DAY.

"IN GOD WE TRUST"

Pastor Ray

DECEMBER 22

DON'T QUIT ASKING

Matt 7:7-8

7 Ask, and it shall be given you; seek, and ye shall find; knock, and it shall be opened unto you: **8** For every one that asketh receiveth; and he that seeketh findeth; and to him that knocketh it shall be opened. KJV

Matt 7:7-8

7 d Keep on asking and it will be given you; **e** keep on seeking and you will find; **f** keep on knocking [reverently] and [the door] will be opened to you. **8** For everyone who keeps on asking receives; and he who keeps on seeking finds; and to him who keeps on knocking, [the door] will be opened. AMP

God wants you to make your need known to Him, He wants you to be straight forward with Him, so don't beat around the bush, speak plain and clear, so that you do not have a misunderstanding, God knows what you need, so get in agreement with Him so He can get it done.

ASK, BELIEVE, AND RECEIVE. HAVE A GREAT DAY.

"IN GOD WE TRUST"

DECEMBER 23

FOLLOW YOUR SHEPHERD

Ps 23

The Lord is my shepherd; I shall not want. **2** He maketh me to lie down in green pastures: he leadeth me beside the still waters. **3** He restoreth my soul: he leadeth me in the paths of righteousness for his name's sake. **4** Yea, though I walk through the valley of the shadow of death, I will fear no evil: for thou art with me; thy rod and thy staff they comfort me. **5** Thou preparest a table before me in the presence of mine enemies: thou anointest my head with oil; my cup runneth over. **6** Surely goodness and mercy shall follow me all the days of my life: and I will dwell in the house of the Lord for ever. KJV

Ps 23

1 THE LORD is my Shepherd [to feed, guide, and shield me], I shall not lack. **2** He makes me lie down in [fresh, tender] green pastures; He leads me beside the still *and* restful waters. [Rev 7:17.] **3** He refreshes *and* restores my life (my self); He leads me in the paths of righteousness [uprightness and right standing with Him—not for my earning it, but] for His name's sake. **4** Yes, though I walk through the [deep, sunless] valley of the shadow of death, I will fear *or* dread no evil, for You are with me; Your rod [to protect] and Your staff [to guide], they comfort me. **5** You prepare a table before me in the presence of my enemies. You anoint my head with **e** oil; my [brimming] cup runs over. **6** Surely *or* only goodness, mercy, *and* unfailing love shall follow me all the days of my life, and through the length of my days the house of the Lord [and His presence] shall be my dwelling place. AMP

FOLLOW JESUS, AND END UP AT HOME IN GOD'S FAMILY.

"IN GOD WE TRUST"

DECEMBER 24

MERRY CHRISTMAS TO ALL

Wishing you all a prosperous, safe and Merry Christmas. My prayers are with you as you travel, for a joyous time with friends and family and a safe return.

The Christmas Story

Luke 2:1-14

1 IN THOSE days it occurred that a decree went out from Caesar Augustus that the whole Roman empire should be registered. 2 This was the first enrollment, and it was made when Quirinius was governor of Syria. 3 And all the people were going to be registered, each to his own city or town. 4 And Joseph also went up from Galilee from the town of Nazareth to Judea, to the town of David, which is called Bethlehem, because he was of the house and family of David,

5 To be enrolled with Mary, his espoused (married) wife, who was about to become a mother. 6 And while they were there, the time came for her delivery,

7 And she gave birth to her Son, her Firstborn; and she wrapped Him in swaddling clothes and laid Him in a manger, because there was no room or place for them in the inn. 8 And in that vicinity there were shepherds living [out under the open sky] in the field, watching [in shifts] over their flock by night.

9 And behold, an angel of the Lord stood by them, and the glory of the Lord flashed and shone all about them, and they were terribly frightened. 10 But the angel said to them, Do not be afraid; for behold, I bring you good news of a great joy which will come to all the people. 11 For to you is born this day in the town of David a Savior, Who is Christ (the Messiah) the Lord! 12 And this will be a sign for you [by which you will recognize Him]: you will find [after searching] a Baby wrapped in swaddling clothes and lying in a manger. 13 Then suddenly there appeared with the angel an army of the troops of heaven (a heavenly knighthood), praising God and saying, 14 Glory to God in the highest [heaven], and on earth peace among men with whom He is well pleased [men of goodwill, of His favor]. AMP

Unto us a Child was born, this is what we celebrate at the Christmas season, then at Easter we celebrate the second half of the prophecy, unto us a Son is given.

THERE WERE 33 YEARS BETWEEN THESE TWO EVENTS.

"IN GOD WE TRUST"

Pastor Ray

DECEMBER 25

MERRY CHRISTMAS

May your day be filled with love and joy, regardless of who you are and where you are, for God has chosen you and given you the gift of life, through His uniquely begotten Son, Jesus, let Him hold you close, to guide and lead you. and fulfill His desire for you.

Luke 2:10-11

10 *And the angel said unto them, Fear not: for, behold, I bring you good tidings of great joy, which shall be to all people.***11** *For unto you is born this day in the city of David a Saviour, which is Christ the Lord.*

3 John 2

2 *Beloved, I wish above all things that thou mayest prosper and be in health, even as thy soul prospereth. KJV*

ENJOY YOUR DAY

"IN GOD WE TRUST"

Pastor Ray

DECEMBER 26

ARE YOU RUNNING A LITTLE LOW?

Proverbs 3:9-10

9 Honour the LORD with thy substance, and with the firstfruits of all thine increase: 10 So shall thy barns be filled with plenty, and thy presses shall burst out with new wine. The King James Version, (Cambridge: Cambridge) 1769.

Prov 3:9-10

9 Honor the Lord with your capital *and* sufficiency [from righteous labors] and with the firstfruits of all your income; [Deut 26:2; Mal 3:10; Luke 14:13,14.] **10** So shall your storage places be filled with plenty, and your vats shall be overflowing with new wine. [Deut 28:8.] AMP

When we honor God, He will honor us, for He wants to be first place in our lives so we can be first place with Him. His main desires is for you to spend time with Him, for where your wealth is there will your heart be also. "Give, and it shall be given unto you; good measure, pressed down, and shaken together, and running over, shall men give into your bosom. For with the same measure that ye mete withal it shall be measured to you again. Luke 6:38 KJV"

GIVE AND IT SHALL BE GIVEN TO YOU. START YOUR NEW YEAR WITH A GIVING HEART.

"IN GOD WE TRUST"

Pastor Ray

DECEMBER 27

UNTO US A CHILD WAS BORN, WHY?

John 10:10

10 The thief cometh not, but for to steal, and to kill, and to destroy: I am come that they might have life, and that they might have it more abundantly. KJV

John 10:10

10 The thief comes only in order to steal and kill and destroy. I came that they may have and enjoy life, and have it in abundance (to the full, till it overflows)

AMP

Gods purpose for bringing Jesus into the world was for us to have a Savior, who paid the price for our sins, a price we could not pay, an example for us to follow in living life to its fullest.

TO LIVE IN THE FULLNESS OF GOD'S BLESSINGS

"IN GOD WE TRUST"

Pastor Ray

DECEMBER 28

BE OF GOOD CHEER

John 16:31-33

31 Jesus answered them, Do ye now believe? **32** Behold, the hour cometh, yea, is now come, that ye shall be scattered, every man to his own, and shall leave me alone: and yet I am not alone, because the Father is with me. **33** These things I have spoken unto you, that in me ye might have peace. In the world ye shall have tribulation: but be of good cheer; I have overcome the world. KJV

Let us enter into the new year with no fear for our future, and His peace in our hearts, and with the good cheer that only His love for us can bring. God knows his plan for us. "(I know what I'm doing. I have it all planned out—plans to take care of you, not abandon you, plans to give you the future you hope for. Jer 29:11 The Message)" Jesus in you, means you are an overcomer, we are told in "1 John 4:4 Ye are of God, little children, and have overcome them: because greater is he that is in you, than he that is in the world." KJV

BE OF GOOD CHEER, FOR JESUS IN YOU HAS OVERCOME THE WORLD.

"IN GOD WE TRUST"

DECEMBER 29

ARE YOU FEELING WEAK?

Ps 29:10-11

10 The Lord sitteth upon the flood; yea, the Lord sitteth King for ever. **11** The Lord will give strength unto his people; the Lord will bless his people with peace. KJV

God will keep you strong and give you peace, if you will allow Him to do so, as He will not make you do anything, you and I have to be willing vessels for Him to use, (in other words His people) if we want to receive these benefits in "(John 14:27 Peace I leave with you, my peace I give unto you: not as the world giveth, give I unto you. *Let not your heart be troubled, neither let it be afraid."* KJV)

RECEIVE HIS PEACE AND BE NOT AFRAID TO ENJOY YOUR DAY.

"IN GOD WE TRUST"

Pastor Ray

DECEMBER 30

DO YOU NEED A HELPER?

Ps 30:10-12

10 Hear, O Lord, and have mercy upon me: Lord, be thou my helper. **11** Thou hast turned for me my mourning into dancing: thou hast put off my sackcloth, and girded me with gladness; **12** To the end that my glory may sing praise to thee, and not be silent. O Lord my God, I will give thanks unto thee for ever. KJV

God always has His ears attuned to your prayers, and His mercy endures forever, His love for you is never ending, with His mercy and love, He will change your sorrow into gladness, your mourning into joy, why?, so that you may enter His gates with praise and thanksgiving. knowing that your helper (the Holy Spirit) has brought you into God's presence, (So we say with confidence, "The Lord is my helper; I will not be afraid. What can man do to me?", Heb 13:6 NIV)

SHOUT WITH JOY, AND HAVE A HAPPY DAY.

"HAPPY NEW YEAR"

"IN GOD WE TRUST"

Pastor Ray

DECEMBER 31

HAPPY NEW YEAR

MY PRAYER FOR YOUR TRIP THROUGH THE NEXT YEAR

1 Cor 1:3-9

3 Grace (favor and spiritual blessing) be to you and [heart] peace from God our Father and the Lord Jesus Christ. **4** I thank my God at all times for you because of the grace (the favor and spiritual blessing) of God which was bestowed on you in Christ Jesus, **5** [So] that in Him in every respect you were enriched, in full power *and* readiness of speech [to speak of your faith] and complete knowledge *and* illumination [to give you full insight into its meaning]. **6** In this way [our] witnessing concerning Christ (the Messiah) was so confirmed *and* established *and* made sure in you **7** That you are not [consciously] falling behind *or* lacking in any special spiritual endowment *or* Christian grace [the reception of which is due to the power of divine grace operating in your souls by the Holy Spirit], while you wait *and* watch [constantly living in hope] for the coming of our Lord Jesus Christ *and* [His] being made visible to all. **8** And He will establish you to the end [keep you steadfast, give you strength, and guarantee your vindication; He will be your warrant against all accusation or indictment so that you will be] guiltless *and* irreproachable in the day of our Lord Jesus Christ (the Messiah). **9** God is faithful (reliable, trustworthy, and therefore ever true to His promise, and He can be depended on); by Him you were called into companionship *and* participation with His Son, Jesus Christ our Lord. AMP

HAVE A HAPPY, PROSPEROUS, AND GREAT NEXT YEAR.

"IN GOD WE TRUST"